SOUTHWEST HOME PLANS

Design 3433, page 9

138 Sun-Loving Designs For Building Anywhere!

- Santa Fe
- Pueblo
- Territorial
- Spanish
- Mediterranean
- Southwest Courtyards

HOME PLANNERS, LLC
Wholly owned by Hanley-Wood, LLC
Tucson, Arizona

Published by Home Planners, LLC
Wholly owned by Hanley-Wood, LLC
Editorial and Corporate Offices:
3275 West Ina Road, Suite 110
Tucson, Arizona 85741

Distribution Center:
29333 Lorie Lane
Wixom, Michigan 48393

Rickard D. Bailey, *CEO and Publisher*
Cindy Coatsworth Lewis, *Director of Publishing*
Paulette Mulvin, *Senior Editor*
Jan Prideaux, *Project Editor*
Paul Fitzgerald, *Senior Graphic Designer*
Karen Leanio, *Graphic Designer*
Michael Shanahan, *Graphic Designer*

Photo Credits
Front Cover: Bob Greenspan
Back Cover: Allen Maertz Photography

First Printing, December, 1996

10 9 8 7 6 5 4

Printed in the United States of America

Library of Congress Catalog Card Number: 96-078881

ISBN softcover: 1-881955-35-4

On the front cover: Design 3433 enjoys a wonderful courtyard that provides room to relax and savor the outdoors. For more information about this design, see page 9.

On the back cover: Design 3405 exhibits the best in Santa Fe style. See page 12 for a closer look.

Design 3643, page 16

TABLE OF CONTENTS

EDITOR'S NOTE: It's true—there's magic in the Southwest! The simple, straightforward appeal of homes steeped in cultural traditions and resourcefulness—combined with a mild climate that promotes the relaxed attitude of a perpetual vacation—are unbeatable. But the magic goes beyond that—and it's easier to experience than explain. So why not experience for yourself the overall sense of contentment and pleasure that begins each day in the home of your dreams—on your own piece of warm-weather paradise! As you'll discover in the chapters that follow, there is a home tailored to fit the lifestyle you deserve—the lifestyle you've dreamed of. To help you plan the cost of your Southwestern dream home, our Quote One® estimating service is available for many of our plans. The Quote One® logo has been placed on the plan pages for easy reference. For additional information regarding this invaluable service, please turn to page 134.

About the Designers

The home plans featured in this book have been created by a diverse group of outstanding home designers and architects. This group of companies is dedicated to creating and marketing the finest possible plans for home construction on a regional and national basis. Each of the companies exhibits superior work and integrity in all phases of the stock-plan business including modern, trendsetting floor planning, a professionally executed blueprint package and a strong sense of service and commitment to the consumer.

Alan Mascord Design Associates, Inc.

Founded in 1983 as a local supplier to the building community, Mascord Design Associates of Portland, Oregon began to successfully publish plans nationally in 1985. With plans now drawn exclusively on computer, Mascord Design Associates quickly received a reputation for homes that are easy to build yet meet the rigorous demands of the buyers' market, winning local and national awards. The company's trademark is creating floor plans that work well and exhibit excellent traffic patterns. Their motto is: "Drawn to build, designed to sell."

Larry W. Garnett & Associates, Inc.

Starting as a designer of homes for Houston-area residents, Garnett & Associates has been marketing designs nationally for the past 15 years. A well-respected design firm, the company's plans are regularly featured in *House Beautiful, Country Living, Home* and *Professional Builder*. Numerous accolades, including several from the Texas Institute of Building Design and the American Institute of Building Design, have been awarded to the company for excellence in architecture.

Home Planners

Headquartered in Tucson, Arizona, with additional offices in Detroit, Home Planners is one of the longest-running and most successful home design firms in the United States. With over 2,500 designs in its portfolio, the company provides a wide range of styles, sizes and types of homes for the residential builder. All of Home Planners designs are created with the care and professional expertise that fifty years of experience in the home-planning business affords. Their homes are designed to be built, lived in and enjoyed for years to come.

Donald A. Gardner, Architects, Inc.

The South Carolina firm of Donald A. Gardner was established in response to a growing demand for residential designs that reflect constantly changing lifestyles. The company's specialty is providing homes with refined, custom-style details and unique features such as passive-solar designs and open floor plans. Computer-aided design and drafting technology resulting in trouble-free construction documents places the firm at the leading edge of the home plan industry.

The Sater Design Collection

The Sater Design Collection has a long established tradition of providing South Florida's most diverse and extraordinary custom designed homes. Their goal is to fulfill each client's particular need for an exciting approach to design by merging creative vision with elements that satisfy a desire for a distinctive lifestyle. This philosophy is proven, as exemplified by over 50 national design awards, numerous magazine features and, most important, satisfied clients. The result is an elegant statement of lasting beauty and value.

Home Design Services

For the past fifteen years, Home Design Services of Florida, has been formulating plans for the sun-country lifestyle. At the forefront of design innovation and imagination, the company has developed award-winning designs that are consistently praised for their highly detailed, free-flowing floor plans, imaginative and exciting interior architecture and elevations which have gained international appeal.

Design Profile, Inc.

With more than twenty years in the design and construction industry, Steve Butcher of Design Profile directs operations for clients in the United States and abroad. The firm specializes in traditional and Southwest home designs with open, flexible floor plans and innovative exteriors. It offers custom design and will modify its stock plans using computer drafting technology.

THE SOUTHWEST—
Warm Welcomes And Cool Styles

From the multi-hued sandstone mesas to the flat lands punctuated with desert foliage, the Southwest inspires homes that reflect the color and essence of the earth.

A graceful blend of Native American and Spanish architectures are found throughout this warm-weather region of America. Strong Spanish influence is no surprise, since a vast portion of what is now the Southwestern United States was controlled by the Spanish from the 17th Century until 1821. And, of course, the Native American peoples, with their strong bond to the earth, have left an influence that speaks for itself.

One of the earliest Spanish-style dwellings in the Southwestern region was the Spanish Colonial. Because of the intense desert climate, these homes were constructed of thick, adobe walls that provided excellent insulation. Very few windows existed, since the preference was for bars, wrought-iron grilles or covered openings, often protected with the spiny ribs of the ocotillo cactus or other materials indigenous to the area.

Because of the warm climate, long porches were built that opened onto courtyards and functioned as sheltered passageways between rooms. Design 9083 (page 115) tenders a bird's-eye view of just such a courtyard. Designed with broad porches and overhanging roofs, these areas offered an umbrella's protection to the pounding monsoon rains of summer and the sun in every season.

In the late 1800s, the Mission-style home came into prominence. Typically, these homes had wide, overhanging eaves and were easily recognized by a mission-type dormer or parapet, traditional elements featured in Design 3628 on page 27.

By the early 1900s, the Pueblo Revival—taking its cue from the ancient Native American dwellings of the Southwest—was well underway. This style was characterized by a stucco exterior and a flat roof with a parapet above irregular rounded edges. Projecting wooden roof beams called vigas extended through the walls. The stepped-back roofline of the original Native American pueblos was often imitated, with window lintels and porches carrying out the hand-crafted theme. Design 3406 (page 14) provides a fine example of the Pueblo Revival style with a Santa Fe flavor.

Between 1915 and 1940, the Spanish Eclectic home made its appearance. The most telling features of these homes are the arches above the windows and doors, and the decorative details inspired by Moorish or Byzantine cultures. See Design 2294 (page 120).

Among the most common terms you may hear in discussions regarding Southwestern architecture are:

Adobe: Mud bricks that have been dried in the sun, but not fired. Traditionally used on a home's exterior, these bricks are covered with a finish coat of plaster or stucco.

Azul Anil: This color—often referred to as Taos Blue—is used on doors to ward off spirits and bring good luck in Mexican and Native American traditions.

Banco: A bench or built-in seat.

Canale: Wood gutters or drain spouts. Typically made from a carved-out log, they project from the corners of an adobe home so water can be carried away from the house.

Latillas: Small wood boards (or sometimes real cactus ribs) that are laid over rafters or beams, creating a lattice-like ceiling finish.

Lintel: Structural support, specifically hewn, used over doorways and windows.

Peredita: A low wall between rooms that stops drafts and directs traffic, yet allows warm air to circulate overhead.

Portale: Simply said, a covered porch.

Saltillo tiles: Large, square, unglazed clay pavers made in Saltillo and other areas of Mexico. Usually red or dark orange, they're used primarily for flooring.

Viga: A beam or rafter, typically an unfinished ponderosa pine log with the bark removed. Vigas often project through adobe walls to the exterior of the home.

While the plans in this book get their roots from Native American and Spanish cultures—they have been updated and filled with amenities that anticipate the needs and desires of today's homeowner. So as you leaf through the pages of this collection, get ready to enjoy and savor the best new home designs the Southwest has to offer!

Design 3431

Square Footage: 1,907

■ Graceful curves welcome you into the courtyard of this Santa Fe home. Inside, a gallery directs traffic to the work zone on the left or the sleeping zone on the right. Straight ahead lies a sunken gathering room with a beam ceiling and a raised-hearth fireplace. A large pantry offers extra storage space for kitchen items. The covered rear porch is accessible from the dining room, gathering room and secluded master bedroom. Luxury describes the feeling in the master bath with a whirlpool tub, a separate shower, a double vanity and lots of closet space. Two family bedrooms share a compartmented bath. The study could serve as a guest room, media room or home office.

QUOTE ONE®

Cost to build? See page 134
to order complete cost estimate
to build this house in your area!

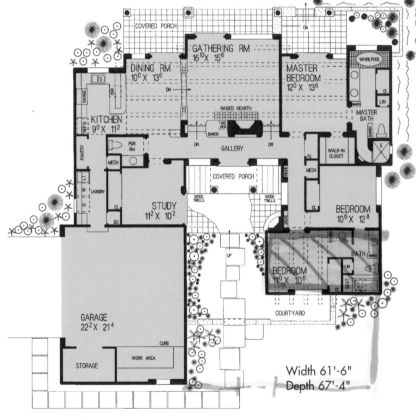

COVERED PORCH

GATHERING RM
16¹⁰ X 15⁶

DINING RM
10⁰ X 13⁶

MASTER BEDROOM
12⁰ X 13⁶

WHIRLPOOL

KITCHEN
9⁰ X 11²

RAISED HEARTH

MASTER BATH

BANCO

WALK-IN CLOSET

GALLERY

PANTRY

PDR RM

MECH

MECH

LAUNDRY

COVERED PORCH

STUDY
11² X 10²

WOOD TRELLS

WOOD TRELLS

BEDROOM
10⁶ X 12⁸

BATH

BEDROOM
11⁰ X 10⁶

GARAGE
22² X 21⁴

UP

COURTYARD

CURB

STORAGE

WORK AREA

Width 61'-6"
Depth 67'-4"

Design by
Home Planners

PUEBLO FRONTIERS

■ This diamond in the desert gives new meaning to old style. Though reminiscent of old Pueblo-type dwellings of the Southwest, the floor plan is anything but ancient history. A cozy courtyard gives way to a long covered porch with nooks for sitting and open-air dining at the front. The double-door entry opens on the right to a gracious living room highlighted by a corner fireplace. Just beyond is the formal dining room with adjacent butler's pantry and access to the porch dining area. To the left of the foyer is a private office with convenient built-ins and attached powder room. The kitchen, family room and morning room separate family bedrooms from the master suite. Both sleeping areas are luxurious with whirlpool spas and separate showers. The master suite also boasts its own exercise room. Though connected to the main house, the guest suite has a private entrance as well, and includes another corner fireplace. Maintain the family fleet in the spacious three-car garage.

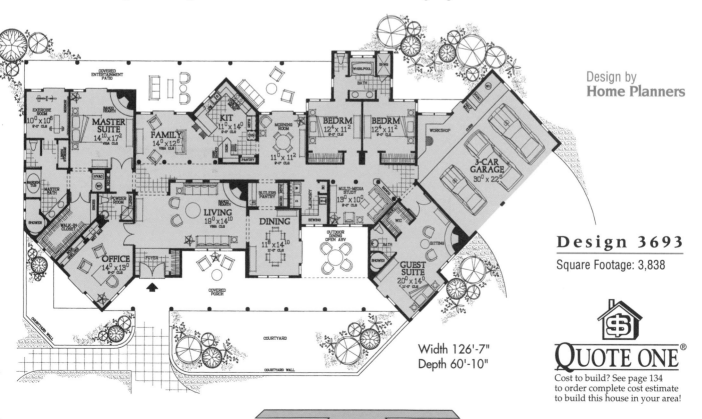

Design by
Home Planners

Design 3693

Square Footage: 3,838

Width 126'-7"
Depth 60'-10"

Design 3642

Square Footage: 2,945

■ Flat roofs, soft, curved wall lines, masses of stucco, exposed rafter tails, an arched privacy wall, carriage lamps and a courtyard are the distinguishing factors of this ranch house. Inside, twin archways provide access to the beam-ceilinged family room. The modified U-shaped kitchen and its breakfast area are open to the family room. The kitchen will be a delight in which to work with its island, pantry and fine counter space. Down the hall are four bedrooms and two baths. Each of the three bedrooms for the children is sizeable and handy to the main bath with its double lavatories. The master suite is outstanding. The master bedroom has fine blank wall areas for flexible furniture placement. It has a view of the patio as well as direct access to it.

Width 73'
Depth 68'-10"

Cost to build? See page 134 to order complete cost estimate to build this house in your area!

This home, as shown in the photograph, may differ from the actual blueprints.
For more detailed information, please check the floor plans carefully.

Photo by Bob Greenspan

Design 3433

Square Footage: 2,350

L

■ Santa Fe styling creates interesting angles in this one-story home. A grand entrance leads through a courtyard into the foyer with a circular skylight, closet space, niches and a convenient powder room. Turn right to the master suite with a deluxe bath and a study close at hand, perfect for a nursery, home office or an exercise room. Two more family bedrooms are placed quietly in the far wing of the house just beyond the family room. Fireplaces in the living room, dining room and on the covered porch create various shapes. Additional amenities include an island range in the kitchen, extra storage in the garage and covered porches on two sides of the house.

Design by
Home Planners

Width 92'-7"
Depth 79'

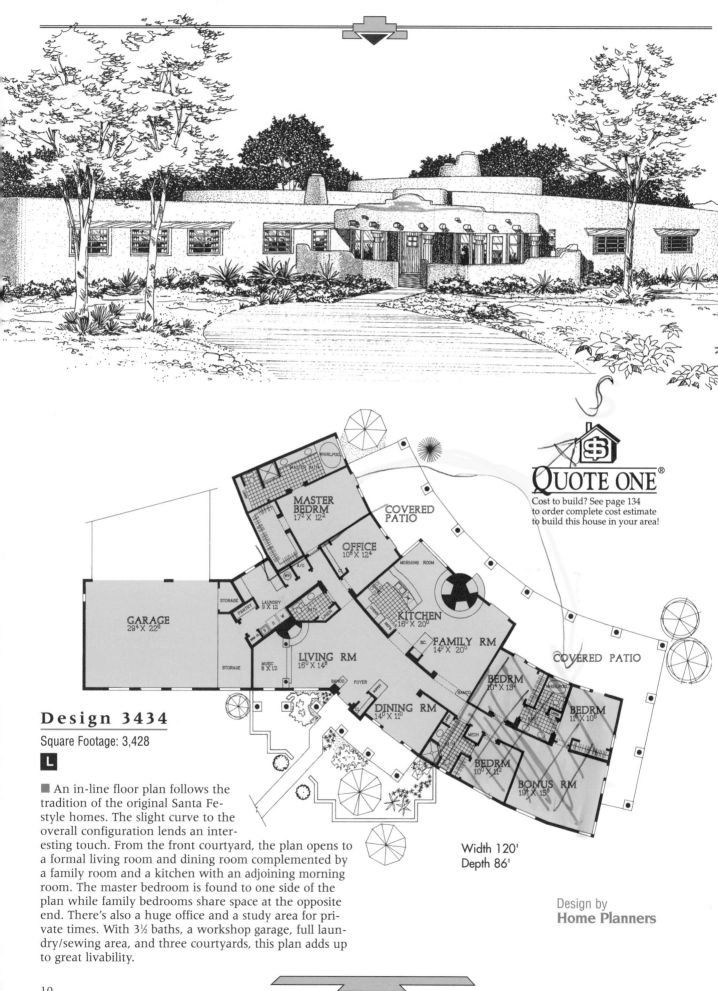

Design 3434

Square Footage: 3,428

L

■ An in-line floor plan follows the
tradition of the original Santa Fe-
style homes. The slight curve to the
overall configuration lends an inter-
esting touch. From the front courtyard, the plan opens to
a formal living room and dining room complemented by
a family room and a kitchen with an adjoining morning
room. The master bedroom is found to one side of the
plan while family bedrooms share space at the opposite
end. There's also a huge office and a study area for private times. With 3½ baths, a workshop garage, full laun-
dry/sewing area, and three courtyards, this plan adds up
to great livability.

Width 120'
Depth 86'

Design by
Home Planners

MASTER BEDRM 17² X 12⁴

COVERED PATIO

OFFICE 10⁶ X 12⁴

MORNING ROOM

GARAGE 29⁴ X 22⁶

STORAGE

PANTRY

LAUNDRY 9 X 12

KITCHEN 16 X 20⁰

FAMILY RM 14⁰ X 20⁰

COVERED PATIO

STORAGE

MUSIC 8 X 12

LIVING RM 16⁰ X 14⁸

BEDRM 10⁴ X 13⁴

BEDRM 11 X 10⁸

FOYER

DINING RM 14⁰ X 11⁰

BEDRM 10⁰ X 11²

BONUS RM 19⁸ X 15⁸

Design 3646

Square Footage: 2,966

■ Here's a rambling ranch with an unique configuration. Massive double doors at the front entrance are sheltered by a covered porch. This well zoned plan offers exceptional one-story livability for the active family. The central foyer routes traffic effectively while featuring a feeling of spaciousness. Note the dramatic columns that accentuate the big living room with its high 17'-8" ceiling. This interesting, angular room has a commanding corner fireplace with a raised hearth, a wall of windows, a doorway to the huge rear covered porch and a pass-through to the kitchen. The informal family room has direct access to the rear porch and is handy to the three children's bedrooms. At the far end of the plan, and guaranteed its full measure of privacy, is the master suite. The master bedroom, with its high ceiling, is large and enjoys direct access to the rear porch.

QUOTE ONE®

Cost to build? See page 134 to order complete cost estimate to build this house in your area!

Design by
Home Planners

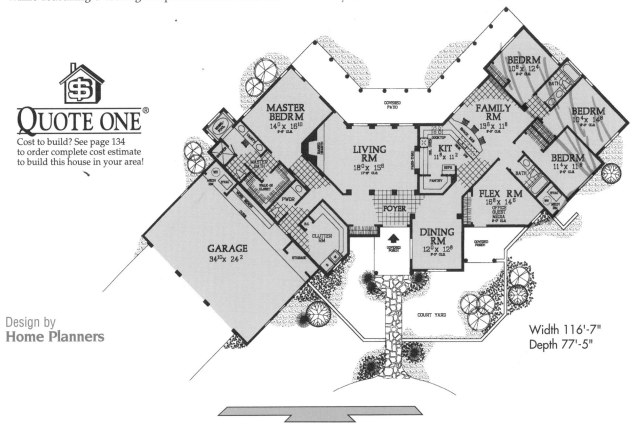

Width 116'-7"
Depth 77'-5"

This home, as shown in the photograph, may differ from the actual blueprints.
For more detailed information, please check the floor plans carefully.

Photo by Allen Maertz Photography

Design 3405

Square Footage: 3,144

■ In classic Santa Fe style, this home strikes a beautiful combination of historic exterior detailing and open floor planning on the inside. A covered porch running the width of the facade leads to an entry foyer that connects to a huge gathering room with a fireplace and a formal dining room. The family kitchen allows special space for casual gatherings. The right wing of the home holds two family bedrooms and a full bath. The left wing is devoted to the master suite and a guest room or a study.

QUOTE ONE®

Cost to build? See page 134
to order complete cost estimate
to build this house in your area!

Design by
Home Planners

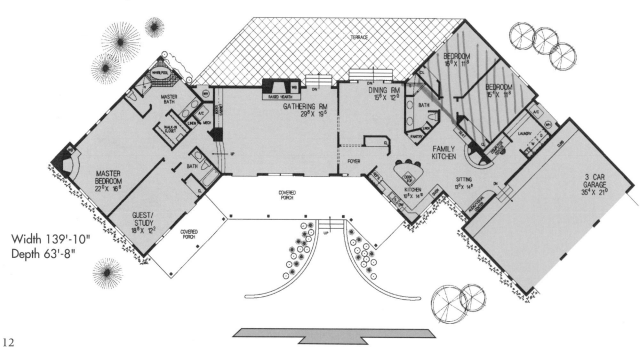

Width 139'-10"
Depth 63'-8"

Design 3329

Square Footage: 3,169

L

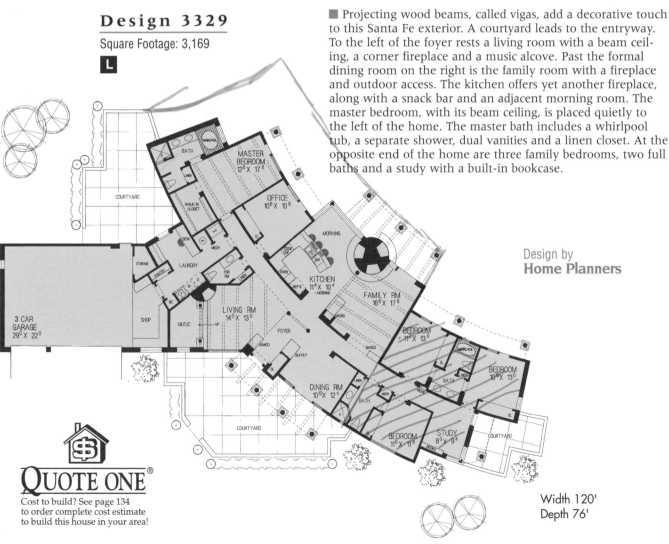

■ Projecting wood beams, called vigas, add a decorative touch to this Santa Fe exterior. A courtyard leads to the entryway. To the left of the foyer rests a living room with a beam ceiling, a corner fireplace and a music alcove. Past the formal dining room on the right is the family room with a fireplace and outdoor access. The kitchen offers yet another fireplace, along with a snack bar and an adjacent morning room. The master bedroom, with its beam ceiling, is placed quietly to the left of the home. The master bath includes a whirlpool tub, a separate shower, dual vanities and a linen closet. At the opposite end of the home are three family bedrooms, two full baths and a study with a built-in bookcase.

Design by
Home Planners

Cost to build? See page 134
to order complete cost estimate
to build this house in your area!

QUOTE ONE®

Width 120'
Depth 76'

Design by
Home Planners

Width 88'-8"
Depth 69'

Design 3406

Square Footage: 2,624

L

■ Angled living spaces add interest to this already magnificent Santa Fe home. From the offset entry you can travel straight back to the open gathering room—or turn to the right to enter the formal living and dining rooms. The huge kitchen is centralized and features an L-shaped work area with an island. Secondary bedrooms open to a side patio and share a full bath. The master suite is complemented by a warm study and is separated from the secondary bedrooms for privacy.

QUOTE ONE®

Cost to build? See page 134
to order complete cost estimate
to build this house in your area!

Design 3644

Square Footage: 2,015

QUOTE ONE®

Cost to build? See page 134
to order complete cost estimate
to build this house in your area!

■ This Santa Fe-style home is as warm as a desert breeze and just as comfortable. Outside details are reminiscent of old-style adobe homes, while the interior caters to convenient living. The front covered porch leads to an open foyer. Columns define the formal dining room and the giant great room. The kitchen has an enormous pantry, a snack bar and is connected to a breakfast nook with rear patio access. Two family bedrooms are found on the right side of the plan. They share a full bathroom with twin vanities. The master suite is on the left side of the plan and has a monstrous walk-in closet and a bath with spa tub and separate shower. The home is completed with a three-car garage.

Width 96'-5"
Depth 54'-9"

Design by
Home Planners

Design 3643

Square Footage: 2,092

L

Stucco exterior walls highlighted by simple window treatment and effective glass-block patterns introduce a fine, western-style home. High ceilings and open planning contribute to the spaciousness of the interior. The large foyer effectively routes traffic to the main living areas. To the left is the angular formal dining room with its half walls and tray ceiling. Straight ahead from the double front doors is the formal living room. It has a high viga, or beamed, ceiling and a commanding corner fireplace with a raised hearth and banco, or bench. It is free of unnecessary cross-room traffic. French doors open to the covered rear patio. Past the built-in bookshelves of the family room is the hallway to the sleeping zone.

Design by
Home Planners

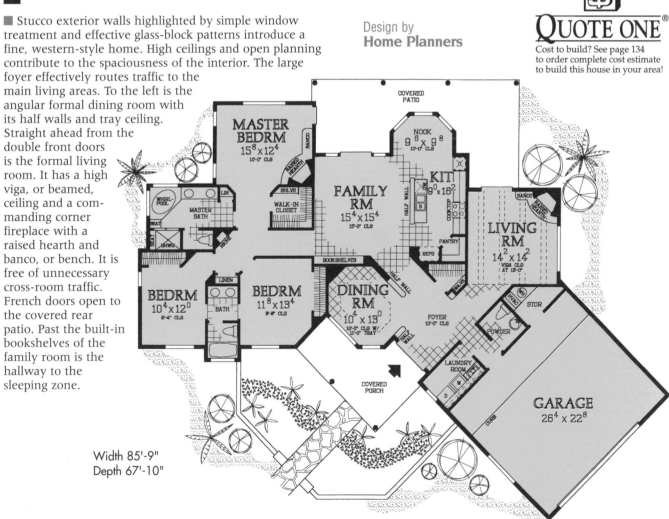

Width 85'-9"
Depth 67'-10"

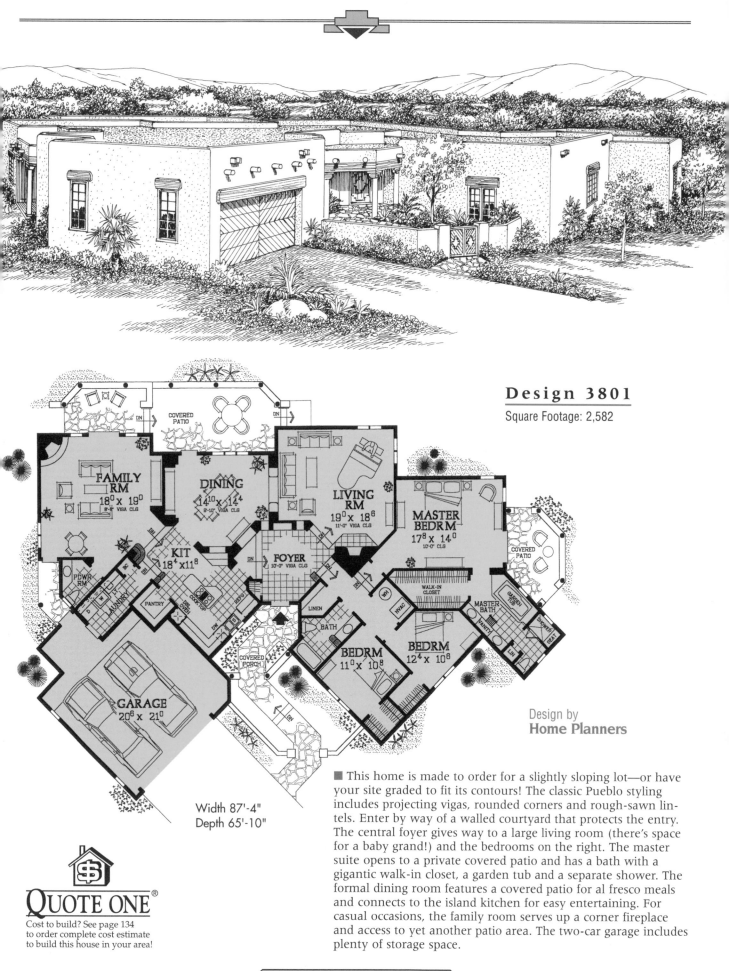

Design 3801

Square Footage: 2,582

FAMILY RM
18⁰ x 19⁰
8'-8" VIGA CLS

DINING
14¹⁰ x 14⁴
9'-10" VIGA CLS

LIVING RM
19⁰ x 18⁶
11'-0" VIGA CLS

MASTER BEDRM
17⁸ x 14⁰
10'-0" CLG

COVERED PATIO

KIT
18⁴ x 11⁸

FOYER
10'-0" VIGA CLS

COVERED PATIO

POWR RM

LAUNDRY

PANTRY

COOK TOP

DW

WALK-IN CLOSET

MASTER BATH

LINEN

BATH

WH

HVAC

GARDEN TUB

BEDRM
11⁰ x 10⁸

BEDRM
12⁴ x 10⁶

GARAGE
20⁸ x 21⁰

COVERED PORCH

Width 87'-4"
Depth 65'-10"

Design by
Home Planners

■ This home is made to order for a slightly sloping lot—or have your site graded to fit its contours! The classic Pueblo styling includes projecting vigas, rounded corners and rough-sawn lintels. Enter by way of a walled courtyard that protects the entry. The central foyer gives way to a large living room (there's space for a baby grand!) and the bedrooms on the right. The master suite opens to a private covered patio and has a bath with a gigantic walk-in closet, a garden tub and a separate shower. The formal dining room features a covered patio for al fresco meals and connects to the island kitchen for easy entertaining. For casual occasions, the family room serves up a corner fireplace and access to yet another patio area. The two-car garage includes plenty of storage space.

QUOTE ONE®

Cost to build? See page 134 to order complete cost estimate to build this house in your area!

Width 75'
Depth 55'

Design 3486

Square Footage: 2,000

■ This classic stucco design provides a cool retreat in any climate. From the covered porch, enter the skylit foyer to find an arched-ceiling leading to the central gathering room with its raised-hearth fireplace and terrace access. A connecting corner dining room is conveniently located near the amenity-filled kitchen that features an abundant pantry, a snack bar and a separate breakfast area. The large master bedroom includes terrace access and a master bath with a whirlpool tub, a separate shower and plenty of closet space. A second bedroom and a study that can be converted to a bedroom complete this wonderful plan.

Design by
Home Planners

Design K115

Square Footage: 3,018

■ Frontal views are no problem with this Southwest pueblo-style home. A large front courtyard with easy access to the main bath easily accommodates pool parties. The entry opens onto the great room with a twelve-foot ceiling and a kiva fireplace, and, further back to the formal dining room through a thick arch and radius wall. An open kitchen, a breakfast room and living room space are ideal for gatherings and also work well with formal areas for entertaining. The kitchen includes an eleven-foot bar and looks out the rear to the covered patio. The master suite is close to the study or home office right off the great room. Bedrooms 2 and 3 share the main bath which can also serve the pool. A three-car garage offers additional storage space. The covered patio covers the entire front of the home, offering a cool shady place to watch desert sunsets.

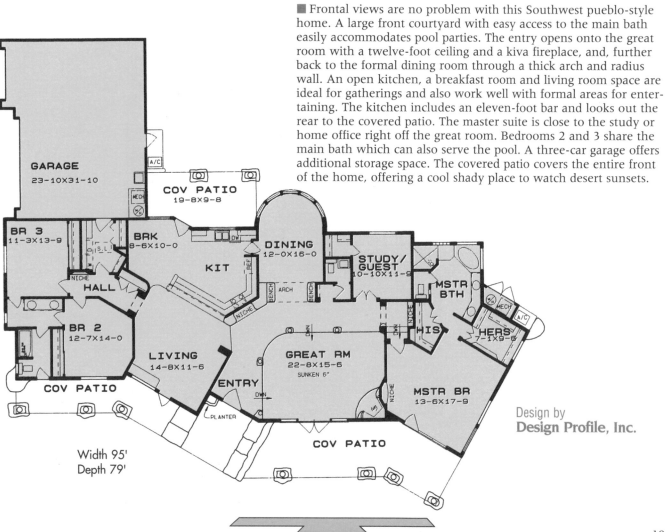

Design by
Design Profile, Inc.

Design 3800

Main Level: 1,946 square feet
Lower Level: 956 square feet
Total: 2,902 square feet

L

Design by
Home Planners

■ The simple, Pueblo-style lines borrowed from the early Native American dwellings combine with contemporary planning for the best possible design. From the front, this home appears to be a one-story. However, a lower level provides a two-story rear elevation, making it ideal for sloping lots. The unique floor plan places a circular staircase to the left of the angled foyer. To the right is an L-shaped kitchen with a walk-in pantry, a sun-filled breakfast room and a formal dining room. Half-walls border the entrance to the formal living room that is warmed by a beehive fireplace. The adjacent covered deck provides shade to the patio below. A roomy master suite, secondary bedroom, full bath and laundry room complete the first floor. The lower level contains a great room, a full bath and two family bedrooms.

Width 51'-6"
Depth 70'-2"

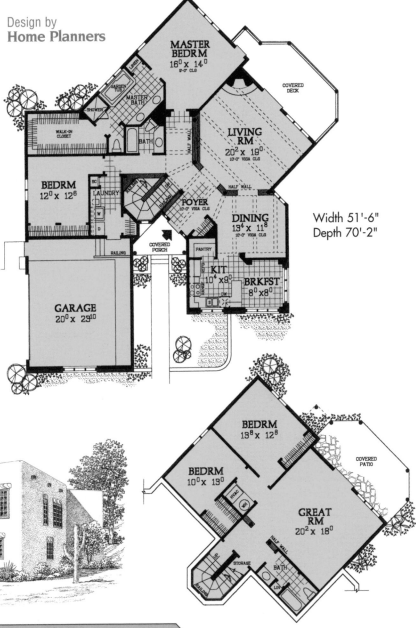

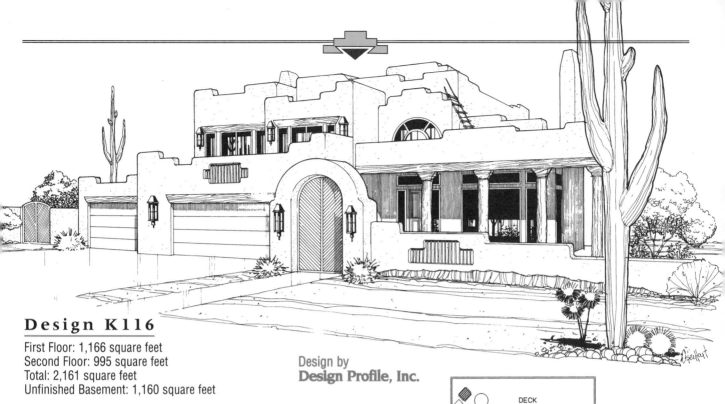

Design K116

First Floor: 1,166 square feet
Second Floor: 995 square feet
Total: 2,161 square feet
Unfinished Basement: 1,160 square feet

Design by
Design Profile, Inc.

■ A blend of territorial and pueblo elements make this a true Southwest style home. You are greeted by a thick, gated archway leading to the front courtyard and a wraparound covered porch. Formal dining and living rooms have eleven-foot ceilings with log vigas and access to the covered patio. The entry showcases an eighteen-foot ceiling and a wood railing staircase to the second floor. The rear family room is open to the kitchen and a breakfast bay that includes a glass door to the large covered patio. Enhancing the kitchen are an island, pantry, and corner sink with corner windows above. The half-bath and laundry are conveniently located with access directly out from the laundry room. The three-car garage offers extra storage space or room for a boat. This plan comes with either a three-bedroom or four-bedroom option! The master features a double-door entry, log viga ceiling beams, and a glass bay with door to a private view deck for lounging. The master bath has double sinks, a corner tub, a separate shower, and a walk-in closet. This plan is available with a basement which includes a large game room, a bedroom, a bath and plenty of storage. Please specify basement or slab foundation when ordering.

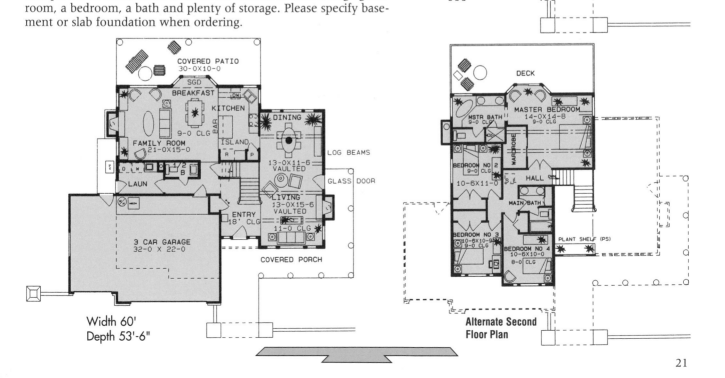

Width 60'
Depth 53'-6"

Alternate Second
Floor Plan

Design 2949

Square Footage: 2,922

■ This one-story matches traditional Southwestern design elements such as stucco, tile, and exposed rafters (called vigas) with an up-to-date floor plan. The 43-foot gathering room provides a dramatic multi-purpose living area. Interesting angles highlight the kitchen, which offers plenty of counter and cabinet space, a planning desk, a snack bar pass-through into the gathering room, and a morning room with a sunny bumped-out bay. The media room could serve as a third bed-room. The luxurious master bed-room contains a walk-in closet and an amenity-filled bath with a whirlpool tub. A three-car garage easily serves the family fleet.

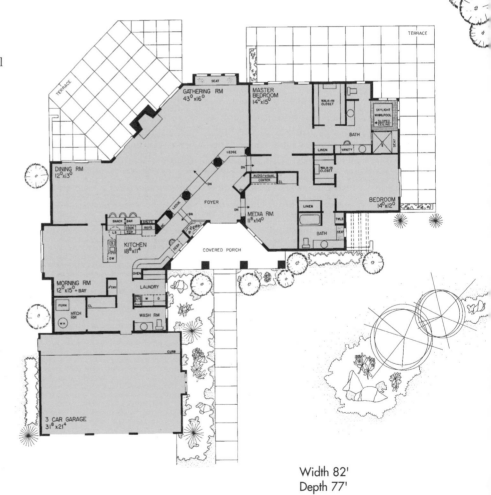

Width 82'
Depth 77'

Cost to build? See page 134 to order complete cost estimate to build this house in your area!

Design by
Home Planners

SANTA FE TERRITORIES

Design 3692

First Floor: 1,911 square feet
Second Floor: 828 square feet
Total: 2,739 square feet

L

Design by
Home Planners

Width 87'-10"
Depth 60'-8"

■ Spanish Colonial design never looked so inviting. This comfortably sized two-story stucco features all the interesting features of Southwestern design: softly curved edges, gentle arches, projecting vigas, free-form composition and a lovely courtyard. The interior holds special livability from the formal dining and living rooms to the more casual family room. Note the circular fireplaces in both the living room and the master bedroom which share one chimney. Covered patios and balconies are abundant in this home, allowing a sense of open space to pervade every room—including all three bedrooms on the second floor.

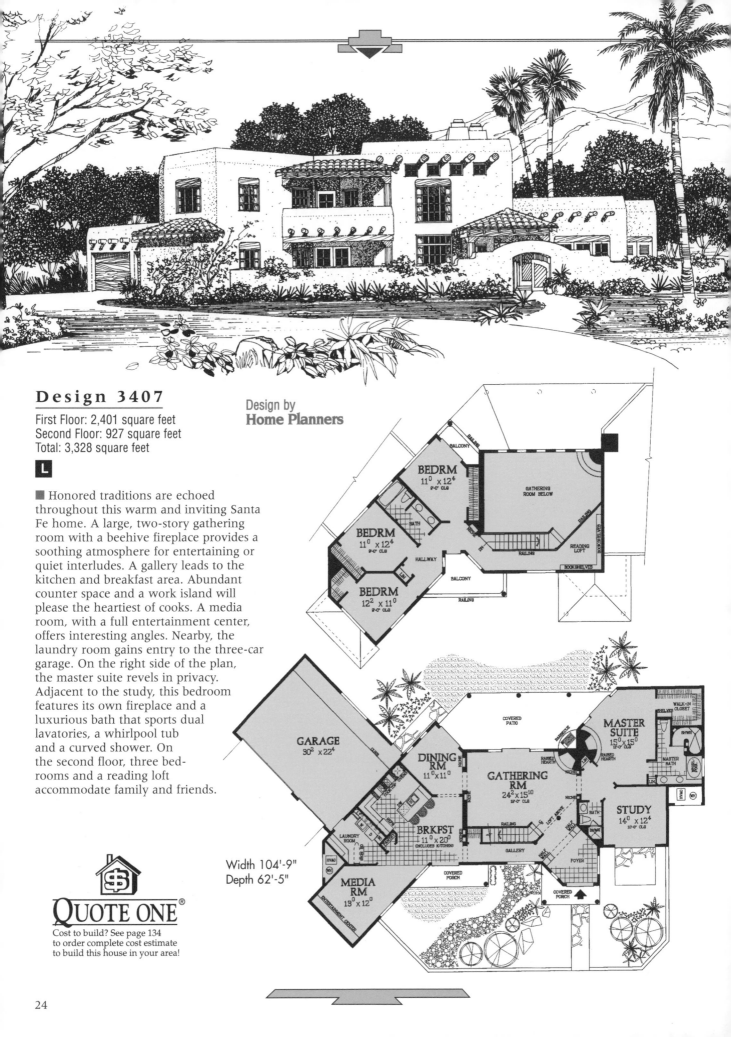

Design 3407

First Floor: 2,401 square feet
Second Floor: 927 square feet
Total: 3,328 square feet

L

Design by
Home Planners

■ Honored traditions are echoed throughout this warm and inviting Santa Fe home. A large, two-story gathering room with a beehive fireplace provides a soothing atmosphere for entertaining or quiet interludes. A gallery leads to the kitchen and breakfast area. Abundant counter space and a work island will please the heartiest of cooks. A media room, with a full entertainment center, offers interesting angles. Nearby, the laundry room gains entry to the three-car garage. On the right side of the plan, the master suite revels in privacy. Adjacent to the study, this bedroom features its own fireplace and a luxurious bath that sports dual lavatories, a whirlpool tub and a curved shower. On the second floor, three bedrooms and a reading loft accommodate family and friends.

Width 104'-9"
Depth 62'-5"

QUOTE ONE®
Cost to build? See page 134
to order complete cost estimate
to build this house in your area!

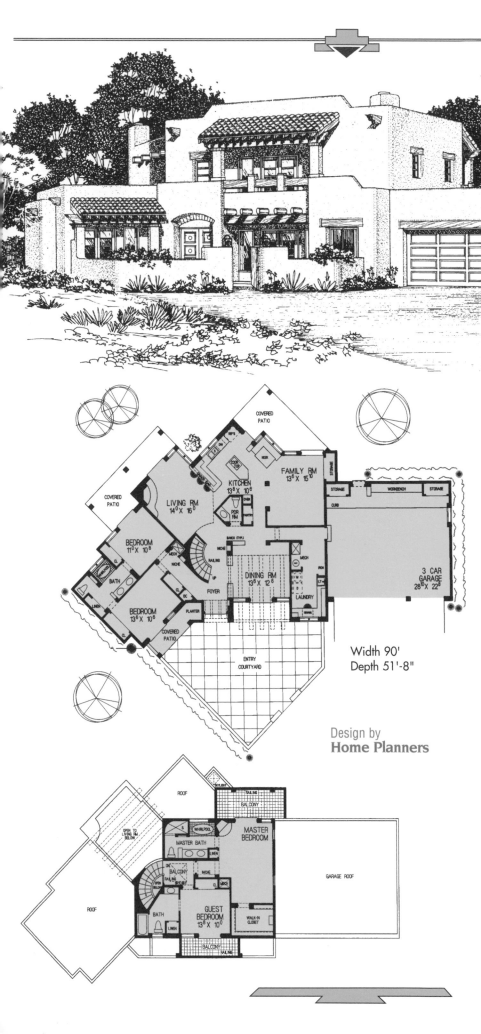

Design 3432

First Floor: 1,966 square feet
Second Floor: 831 square feet
Total: 2,797 square feet

L

■ Unique in nature, this two-story Santa Fe-style home is as practical as it is lovely. The entry foyer leads past a curving staircase to living areas at the back of the plan. These include a living room with a corner fireplace and a family room connected to the kitchen via a built-in eating nook. The kitchen furthers its appeal with an island cooktop and a snack bar. Two family bedrooms on this level include one with a private covered patio. They share a full bath with dual lavatories and a whirlpool. Upstairs, the master suite features a grand bath, a corner fireplace, a large walk-in closet and a private balcony. A guest bedroom accesses a full bath. Every room in this home has its own outdoor area.

Width 90'
Depth 51'-8"

Design by
Home Planners

Cost to build? See page 134
to order complete cost estimate
to build this house in your area!

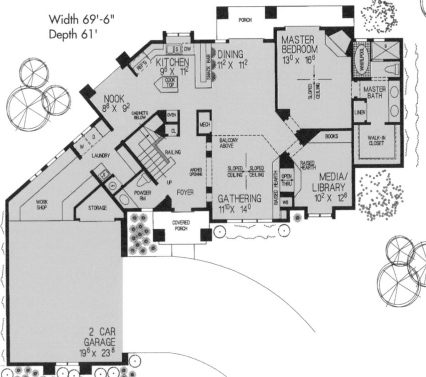

Width 69'-6"
Depth 61'

PORCH

KITCHEN
9⁶ X 11²

REF'G

S DW

DINING
11² X 11²

SNACK BAR

MASTER
BEDROOM
13⁰ X 16⁸

WHIRLPOOL

MASTER
BATH

NOOK
8⁸ X 9²

COOK
TOP

CABINETS
BELOW

OVEN

CL

MECH

LINEN

W D
W D

LAUNDRY

RAILING

BALCONY
ABOVE

BOOKS

WALK-IN
CLOSET

ARCHED
OPENING

UP

SLOPED
CEILING

SLOPED
CEILING

RAISED
HEARTH

WORK
SHOP

POWDER
RM

FOYER

GATHERING
11¹⁰ X 14⁰

OPEN
THRU

MEDIA/
LIBRARY
10² X 12⁸

STORAGE

RAISED HEARTH

WB

COVERED
PORCH

2 CAR
GARAGE
19⁶ x 23⁸

Cost to build? See page 134
to order complete cost estimate
to build this house in your area!

Design 3437

First Floor: 1,522 square feet
Second Floor: 800 square feet
Total: 2,322 square feet

L

Design by
Home Planners

■ This two-story Spanish Mission-style home has character
inside and out. The first-floor master suite features a fireplace and a gracious bath with a walk-in closet, a whirlpool,
a shower, dual vanities and linen storage. The kitchen, with
an island cooktop, includes a snack bar and an adjoining
breakfast nook, and offers a snack bar pass-through into the
formal dining room. The gathering room shares the warmth
of a raised-hearth fireplace with the cozy media/library
room complete with built-in bookshelves. Three bedrooms
and two full baths occupy the second floor.

GUEST
BEDROOM
10⁰ X 11⁰

BEDROOM
10⁶ X 11⁰

CL

LINEN

S

BATH

CL

BATH

DN

BALCONY

RAILING

MECH

CL

OPEN TO
BELOW

OPEN TO
GATHERING RM
BELOW

BEDROOM
11² X 10⁴

Width 90'-2"
Depth 69'-10"

■ Varying roof planes of colorful tile surfaces make a dramatic statement. Privacy fences add appeal and help form the front courtyard and side private patio. Nine-foot ceilings enhance the feeling of spaciousness inside. The kitchen has an island cooktop, built-in ovens, a nearby walk-in pantry and direct access to the outdoor covered patio. The living room is impressive with its a centered fireplace with long raised hearth. The ceiling is eighteen-feet high and permits a fine view of the second-floor loft. It, too, functions through French doors with the rear patio. At the opposite end of the plan is the master bedroom. It has a walk-in closet with shoe storage, twin lavatories in the bath, plus a whirlpool and stall shower. Not to be overlooked is the access to the private patio and the rear patio. The two children's bedrooms each have direct access to a bath with twin lavatories.

Design 3628

First Floor: 1,731 square feet
Second Floor: 554 square feet
Total: 2,285 square feet

Quote One®
Cost to build? See page 134
to order complete cost estimate
to build this house in your area!

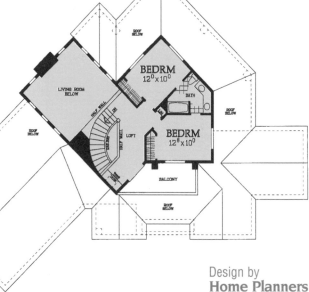

Design by
Home Planners

27

Design 3645

First Floor: 2,024 square feet
Second Floor: 800 square feet
Total: 2,824 square feet

L

■ Tame the wild west with this handsome adobe-style home. Suitable for side-sloping lots, it contains a wealth of livability. A beehive fireplace graces the living room to enhance formal entertaining. The formal dining room is nearby. An office or TV room is located near the master bedroom suite. All will enjoy the family room, which opens to outdoor spaces. Three secondary bedrooms include a guest room with its own bath. Split styling puts the master bedroom suite on the right side of the plan. Here, a walk-in closet, a curved shower and dual vanities bring a touch of luxury.

Width 80'-10"
Depth 54'

Design by
Home Planners

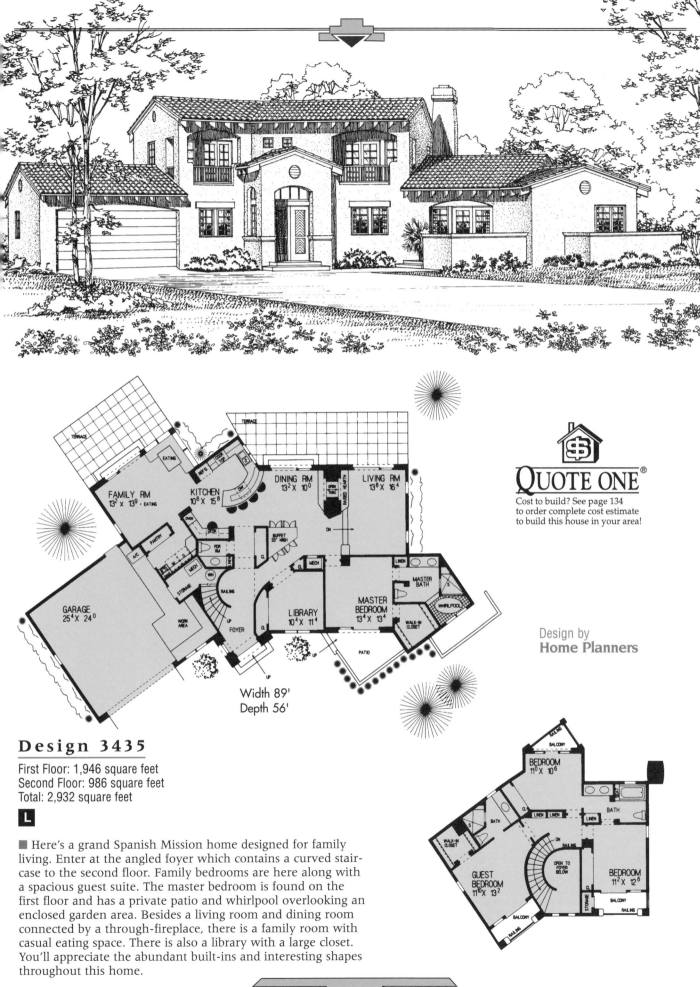

Quote One®

Cost to build? See page 134
to order complete cost estimate
to build this house in your area!

Design by
Home Planners

Width 89'
Depth 56'

Design 3435

First Floor: 1,946 square feet
Second Floor: 986 square feet
Total: 2,932 square feet

L

■ Here's a grand Spanish Mission home designed for family living. Enter at the angled foyer which contains a curved staircase to the second floor. Family bedrooms are here along with a spacious guest suite. The master bedroom is found on the first floor and has a private patio and whirlpool overlooking an enclosed garden area. Besides a living room and dining room connected by a through-fireplace, there is a family room with casual eating space. There is also a library with a large closet. You'll appreciate the abundant built-ins and interesting shapes throughout this home.

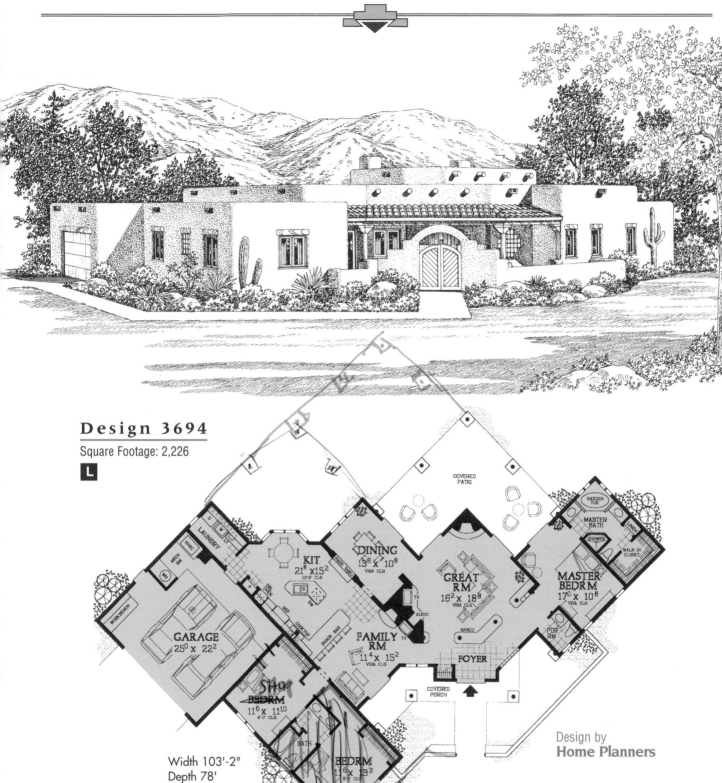

Design 3694

Square Footage: 2,226

L

Width 103'-2"
Depth 78'

Design by
Home Planners

■ The impressive, double-door entry to the walled courtyard sets the tone for this Santa Fe masterpiece home. The expansive living room shows off its casual style with a centerpiece fireplace and abundant windows overlooking the patio. Joining the living room is the formal dining room, again graced with windows and patio doors. The large gourmet kitchen has an eat-in snack bar and joins the family room to create a warm atmosphere for casual entertaining. Family room extras include a fireplace, entertainment built-ins and double doors to the front courtyard. Just off the family room are the two large family bedrooms, which share a private bath. The relaxing master suite is privately located off the living room and has double doors to the back patio.

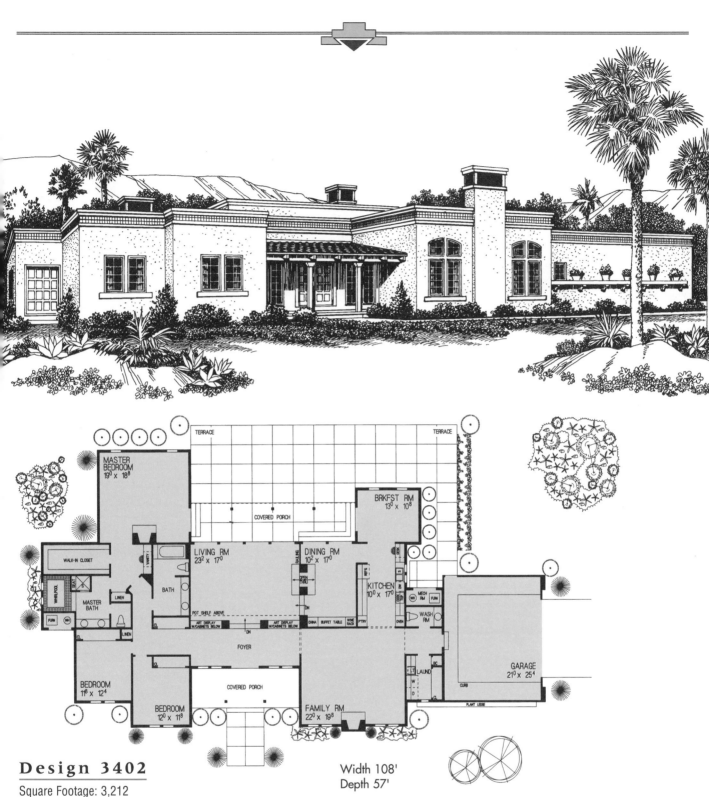

Design 3402

Square Footage: 3,212

L

■ This one-story home pairs the customary tile and stucco of Spanish design with a very livable floor plan. The sunken living room with its open-hearth fireplace promises to be a cozy gathering place. For more casual occasions, there's a welcoming family room with a fireplace off the foyer. The kitchen works well with the formal dining room and nearby breakfast room which offers access to the rear terrace. Two secondary bedrooms share a large full hall bath while a sumptuous master suite enjoys a huge walk-in closet, a whirlpool tub, a separate shower and a romantic fireplace.

Width 108'
Depth 57'

Design by
Home Planners

Design by
Home Planners

Design 3401

Square Footage: 2,850

L

Width 86'
Depth 69'

■ This Southwestern design caters to families who enjoy outdoor living and entertaining. Doors open onto a shaded terrace from the master bedroom and living room, while a sliding glass door in the family room accesses a smaller terrace. Outdoor entertaining is a breeze with the outdoor bar with pass-through window to the kitchen. In the sleeping wing, two secondary bedrooms share a hall bath with a dual-bowl vanity, while the master suite is designed to pamper the fortunate homeowner with such amenities as a corner fireplace, His and Hers walk-in closets, a whirlpool tub, a separate shower and a separate vanity.

QUOTE ONE®

Cost to build? See page 134 to order complete cost estimate to build this house in your area!

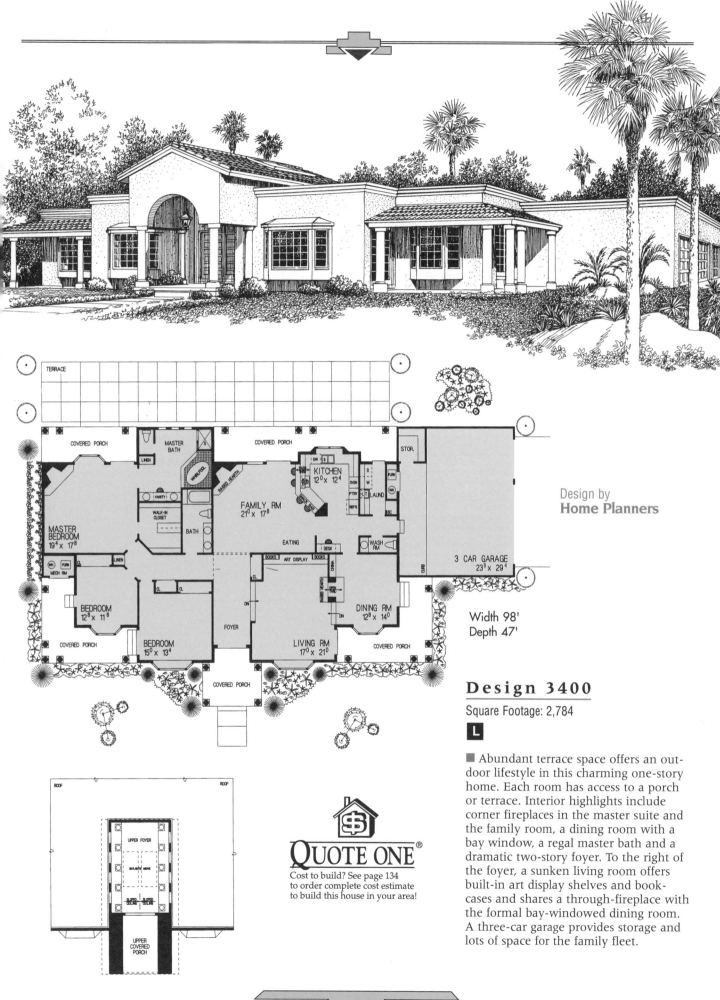

TERRACE

COVERED PORCH

MASTER BATH

LINEN

COVERED PORCH

STOR.

KITCHEN
12⁰ x 12⁴

Design by
Home Planners

WHIRLPOOL

VANITY

RAISED HEARTH

FAMILY RM
21⁰ x 17⁸

DW S

OVEN

D
W

FURN

MASTER
BEDROOM
19⁴ x 17⁸

WALK-IN
CLOSET

BATH

EATING

PTRY CLT LAUND

REF'G

WH

TBC

3 CAR GARAGE
23⁸ x 29⁴

WH FURN

MECH RM

LINEN

BOOKS

ART DISPLAY

BOOKS

DESK

WASH RM

CL

BOOKS

CL

CL

DN

DINING RM
12⁸ x 14⁰

BEDROOM
12⁸ x 11⁸

RAISED HEARTH

OPEN SHELF

CHINA

DN

Width 98'
Depth 47'

BEDROOM
15⁰ x 13⁴

FOYER

LIVING RM
17⁰ x 21⁰

COVERED PORCH

COVERED PORCH

COVERED PORCH

COVERED PORCH

Design 3400

Square Footage: 2,784

L

■ Abundant terrace space offers an outdoor lifestyle in this charming one-story home. Each room has access to a porch or terrace. Interior highlights include corner fireplaces in the master suite and the family room, a dining room with a bay window, a regal master bath and a dramatic two-story foyer. To the right of the foyer, a sunken living room offers built-in art display shelves and bookcases and shares a through-fireplace with the formal bay-windowed dining room. A three-car garage provides storage and lots of space for the family fleet.

ROOF

ROOF

UPPER FOYER

SKYLIGHT ABOVE

SLOPED CEILING SLOPED CEILING

UPPER
COVERED
PORCH

QUOTE ONE®

Cost to build? See page 134 to order complete cost estimate to build this house in your area!

Design 3630

Square Footage: 3,034

L

Design by
Home Planners

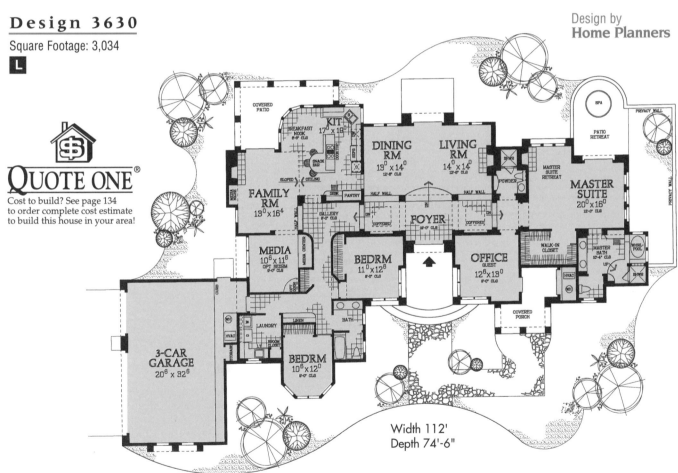

QUOTE ONE®

Cost to build? See page 134
to order complete cost estimate
to build this house in your area!

Width 112'
Depth 74'-6"

■ A grand entry enhances the exterior of this elegant stucco home. The office located at the front of the plan makes this design ideal for a home-based business. Formal areas combine to provide lots of space for entertaining. The kitchen, complete with a snack bar and a breakfast nook, opens to the family room which connects to the media room. The private master suite includes two retreats—one is a multi-windowed sitting area, the other contains a spa for outdoor enjoyment. A walk-in closet and a luxurious bath complete this area. Two family bedrooms share a full bath.

SOUTHWEST CONTEMPORARIES

Design by
Home Planners

Design 3639

First Floor: 2,137 square feet
Second Floor: 671 square feet
Total: 2,808 square feet

L

QUOTE ONE®
Cost to build? See page 134
to order complete cost estimate
to build this house in your area!

Width 75'-6"
Depth 62'-6"

■ If first impressions really make the most important
statements—this home makes it in grand style. The two-
story entry and double doors to the reception foyer make
a first impression that can't be beat. Inside, formal living
areas grab your attention with a dining room and an elegant living room that opens to a covered entertainment
area outside. The family room—with a fireplace—features
open views to the kitchen and breakfast nook. The nearby "recipe corner" includes a built-in desk. The laundry
room is fully functional with a laundry tub and a broom
closet. On the left side of the plan, the master bedroom
suite has a full, private bath and a lanai perfect for a spa.
A large den could easily double as a study. Two bedrooms
and a full bath are located upstairs.

Design 3449

First Floor: 1,336 square feet
Second Floor: 1,186 square feet
Total: 2,522 square feet

Design by
Home Planners

L

■ A covered porch leads inside this home's angled entry to a wide, tiled foyer. A curving staircase makes an elegant impression in the open space encompassing the living and dining rooms with two-story ceilings. A through-fire-place warms the nook and family room with wet bar and glass shelves. The nook also includes planters on two sides. Upstairs, light spills into the whirlpool tub in the master bath with dual vanities and a walk-in closet. The master bedroom includes a sitting area, two more closets and access to a private covered deck. Two family bedrooms share a full bath with dual vanities.

Width 58'-9"
Depth 54'-10"

QUOTE ONE®

Cost to build? See page 134
to order complete cost estimate
to build this house in your area!

Photo by Bob Greenspan

This home, as shown in the photograph, may differ from the actual blueprints. For more detailed information, please check the floor plans carefully.

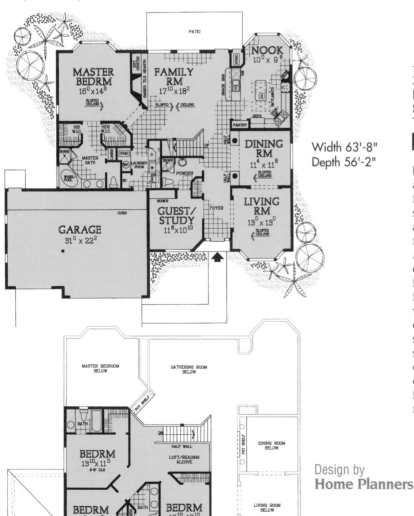

Width 63'-8"
Depth 56'-2"

Design by
Home Planners

Design 3441

First Floor: 2,022 square feet
Second Floor: 845 square feet
Total: 2,867 square feet

L

■ Special details make the difference between a house and this two-story home. A two-story foyer ushers you into a comfortable layout. A snack bar, an audio-visual center, a fireplace and a high, sloped ceiling make the family room a favorite place for informal gathering. A desk, an island cooktop, a bay and skylights enhance the kitchen area. The dining room features two columns and a plant ledge. The formal living room is graced by a sunny bay window, while across the hall a cozy study encourages quiet times. The first-floor master suite includes His and Hers walk-in closets, a spacious bath and a bay window. On the second floor, one bedroom features a walk-in closet and private bath which makes it perfect for a guest suite, while two additional bedrooms share a full bath.

QUOTE ONE®

Cost to build? See page 134 to order complete cost estimate to build this house in your area!

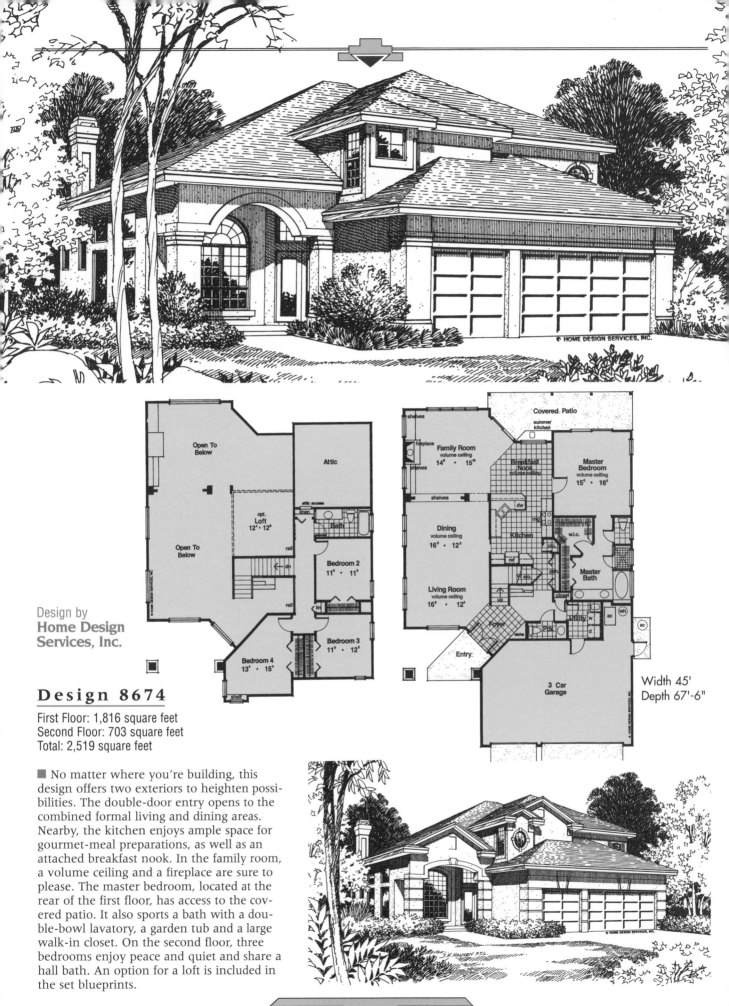

Design by
Home Design
Services, Inc.

Design 8674

First Floor: 1,816 square feet
Second Floor: 703 square feet
Total: 2,519 square feet

Width 45'
Depth 67'-6"

■ No matter where you're building, this design offers two exteriors to heighten possibilities. The double-door entry opens to the combined formal living and dining areas. Nearby, the kitchen enjoys ample space for gourmet-meal preparations, as well as an attached breakfast nook. In the family room, a volume ceiling and a fireplace are sure to please. The master bedroom, located at the rear of the first floor, has access to the covered patio. It also sports a bath with a double-bowl lavatory, a garden tub and a large walk-in closet. On the second floor, three bedrooms enjoy peace and quiet and share a hall bath. An option for a loft is included in the set blueprints.

Width 52'
Depth 64'-4"

Design by
Home Planners

Design 3425

First Floor: 1,776 square feet
Second Floor: 1,035 square feet
Total: 2,811 square feet

■ Here's a two-story Spanish design with an appealing, angled exterior. Inside is an interesting floor plan containing rooms with a variety of shapes. Formal areas are to the right of the entry tower: a sunken living room with a fireplace and a large dining room with access to the rear porch. The kitchen has loads of counter space and is complemented by a bumped-out breakfast room. Note the second fireplace in the family room and the first-floor bedroom which could also be a guest suite. Three second-floor bedrooms radiate around the upper foyer, including the deluxe master suite. Among its many amenities; a private balcony, a walk in closet and a sumptuous bath.

Design 3403

First Floor: 2,422 square feet
Second Floor: 714 square feet
Total: 3,136 square feet

L

■ There is no end to the distinctive features in this Southwestern contemporary home. Formal living areas are concentrated in the center of the plan, perfect for entertaining. To the right of the plan, the kitchen and family room function well together as an informal living area. There is also a separate laundry room nearby. The optional guest bedroom or den and the master bedroom are located to the left of the plan. Upstairs, the remaining two bedrooms are reached by a balcony overlooking the living room and share a bath with twin vanities.

QUOTE ONE®

Cost to build? See page 134
to order complete cost estimate
to build this house in your area!

Width 77'-8"
Depth 62'

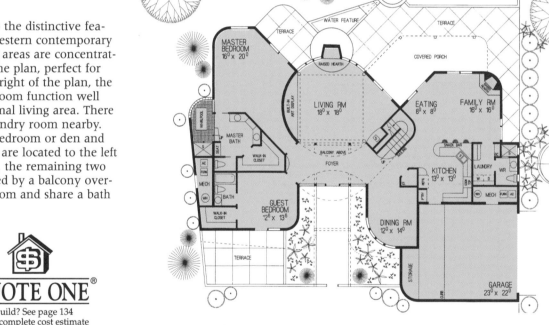

Design by
Home Planners

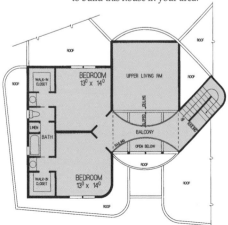

Design 3409

First Floor: 1,481 square feet
Second Floor: 1,287 square feet
Total: 2,768 square feet

L

QUOTE ONE®

Cost to build? See page 134
to order complete cost estimate
to build this house in your area!

Width 64'
Depth 56'-2"

PATIO

COVERED PORCH

FAMILY RM
24⁰ X 15⁴

EATING

DESK

KITCHEN
14⁸ X 15⁸
• EATING

GLASS
BLOCK

OPEN THRU
FIREPLACE

OPEN
TO
ABOVE

UP

SNACK
BAR

COOK
TOP

REF.

FURN.

WH

MECH.

VAULTED
CEILING

BARREL
VAULTED
CEILING

WET BAR

PANTRY

LAUNDRY

W

D

STORAGE

LIVING RM
15⁶ X 15²

FOYER

PDR
RM

BC

WH

FURN.

DINING RM
12⁰ X 10¹⁰

COVERED PATIO

STEPPED
CLG.

CURB

2 CAR
GARAGE
21⁸ X 21⁸
• STORAGE

STORAGE

GLASS BLOCK

MASTER
BATH

VANITY

WHIRLPOOL

DECK

RAILING

BEDROOM
10⁸ X 11²

WALK-IN
CLOSET

LIN

BATH

MASTER
BEDROOM
15¹⁰ X 13⁶

SEAT

RAILING

OPEN TO
BELOW

DN

BEDROOM
10⁸ X 10¹⁰

OPEN TO
PLANTER
BELOW

LEDGE

OPEN TO
FOYER
BELOW

BEDROOM
10⁸ X 10¹⁰

OPEN TO
LIVING RM
BELOW

FLAT
ROOF

ROOF

ROOF

Design by
Home Planners

■ Glass block walls and a foyer with a barrel vaulted ceiling create an interesting exterior. Covered porches to the front and rear provide for excellent indoor/outdoor living relationships. Inside, a large planter and through-fireplace enhance the living room and family room. A desk, eating area and a snack bar are special features in the kitchen. Upstairs, the master suite is highlighted by a large walk-in closet, a bath with a separate shower and tub, and a private deck. Three additional bedrooms share a full bath.

Design 3565

First Floor: 1,248 square feet
Second Floor: 1,012 square feet
Total: 2,260 square feet

L **D**

QUOTE ONE®

Cost to build? See page 134
to order complete cost estimate
to build this house in your area!

DINING RM.
10⁸ x 11⁴

FAMILY RM.
13⁰ x 20⁰

KITCHEN
10⁰ x 13⁴

COOK TOP

OVEN

LIVING RM.
14⁸ x 15⁰

FOYER
OPEN ABOVE

PDR. RM.

STUDY
13⁴ x 11⁰

PORCH

CURB

3-CAR GARAGE
31⁴ x 21⁸

Width 59'-4"
Depth 58'-8"

MASTER BED RM.
13⁰ x 20⁰

SEAT

WHIRLPOOL

SHLVS.

DRSG.

W.I.C.

BALCONY

VAN.

CL.

DN

LINEN

UPPER FOYER

BATH

BED RM.
12⁰ x 12⁸

BED RM.
11⁰ x 10⁴

■ Every detail of this plan speaks of contemporary design. The exterior is simple yet
elegant, while interior floor planning is
thorough yet efficient. The formal living and
dining rooms are to the left of the foyer,
separated by columns. The living room features a wall of windows and a fireplace. The
kitchen, with its island cooktop is adjacent
to the large family room with terrace access.
A private study with additional terrace
access completes the first floor. The master
bedroom features a balcony and a spectacular bath with a whirlpool tub, a shower with
a seat, separate vanities and a walk-in closet.
Two family bedrooms share a full bath.

This home, as shown in the photograph, may differ from the actual blueprints.
For more detailed information, please check the floor plans carefully.

Photo by Andrew D. Lautman

Design 3414

First Floor: 2,024 square feet
Second Floor: 1,144 square feet
Total: 3,168 square feet

L

■ Though seemingly compact from the exterior, this home gives a definite feeling of spaciousness inside. The two-story entry connects directly to a formal living/dining area, a fitting complement to the more casual family room and cozy, bayed breakfast room. Located on the first floor for privacy, the master suite is luxury defined. A bayed sitting area, His and Hers walk-in closets, a whirlpool tub and twin vanities all combine to provide a lavish retreat. Upstairs, three family bedrooms share a full hall bath, while a large guest room waits to pamper with its private bath and access to its own deck. A three-car garage will protect both the family fleet and visitor's vehicles.

Design by
Home Planners

Width 57'
Depth 64'

Cost to build? See page 134
to order complete cost estimate
to build this house in your area!

Design 3429

First Floor: 1,739 square feet
Second Floor: 1,376 square feet
Total: 3,115 square feet

L

■ From the dramatic open entry to the covered back porch, this home delivers a full measure of livability in Spanish design. Formal living areas (living room and dining room) have a counterpoint in the family room and glassed-in breakfast room. The kitchen is a hub for both areas. The first floor study has an adjacent bath, making it a fine guest room when needed. On the second floor, the activities room with built-ins serves two family bedrooms and a grand master suite. The master suite is designed for pampering with a bayed sitting area, a large walk-in closet and a sumptuous bath.

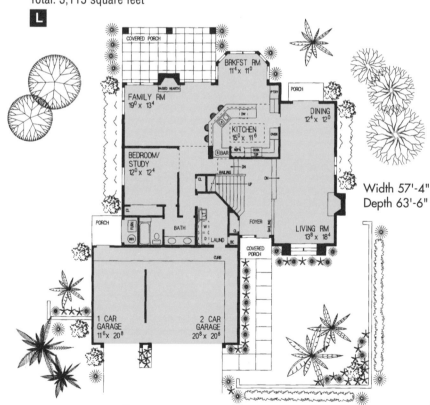

Width 57'-4"
Depth 63'-6"

Design by
Home Planners

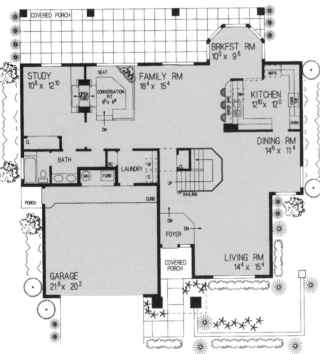

Width 54'
Depth 55'-4"

Design 3424

First Floor: 1,625 square feet
Second Floor: 982 square feet
Total: 2,607 square feet

L

■ You'll find plenty about this Spanish design that will
delight you and your family. Enjoy indoor/outdoor living
in the gigantic family room with covered patio access and
a sunken conversation area sharing a through-fireplace
with the study. An L-shaped kitchen has an attached,
glass-surrounded breakfast room and is conveniently
located next to the formal dining room/living room combination. The second floor contains an opulent master
suite that shares the warmth of a fireplace with its relaxing master bath. Two family bedrooms and a full bath are
also found on this floor.

Design 3563

First Floor: 1,023 square feet
Second Floor: 866 square feet
Total: 1,889 square feet

L **D**

■ Practical to build, this wonderful transitional plan combines the best of contemporary and traditional styling. Its stucco exterior is enhanced by arched windows and a recessed arched entry plus a lovely balcony off the second-floor master bedroom. A walled entry court extends the living room on the outside. The double front doors open to a foyer with a hall closet and a powder room. The service entrance is just to the right and accesses the two-car garage. The large living room adjoins directly to the dining room. The family room is set off behind the garage and features a sloped ceiling and a fireplace. Sleeping quarters consist of two secondary bedrooms with a shared bath and a generous master suite with a well-appointed bath.

Width 52'-4"
Depth 34'-8"

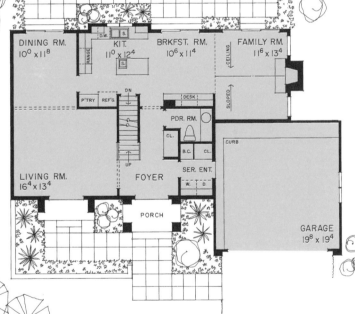

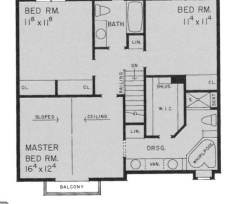

QUOTE ONE®

Cost to build? See page 134
to order complete cost estimate
to build this house in your area!

Design by
Home Planners

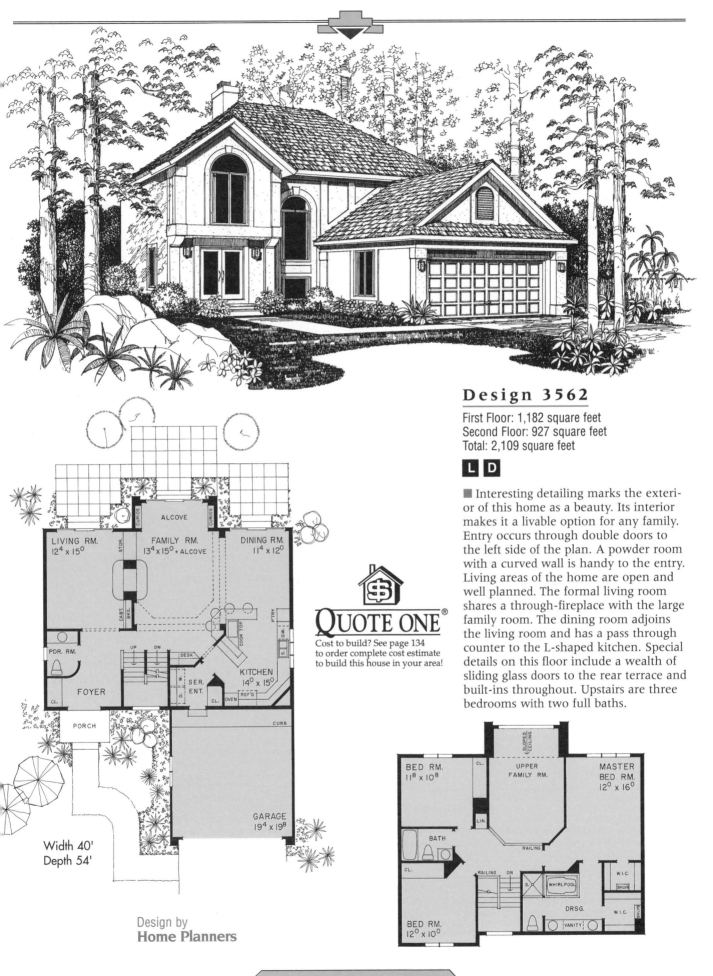

Design 3562

First Floor: 1,182 square feet
Second Floor: 927 square feet
Total: 2,109 square feet

L **D**

■ Interesting detailing marks the exterior of this home as a beauty. Its interior makes it a livable option for any family. Entry occurs through double doors to the left side of the plan. A powder room with a curved wall is handy to the entry. Living areas of the home are open and well planned. The formal living room shares a through-fireplace with the large family room. The dining room adjoins the living room and has a pass through counter to the L-shaped kitchen. Special details on this floor include a wealth of sliding glass doors to the rear terrace and built-ins throughout. Upstairs are three bedrooms with two full baths.

QUOTE ONE®

Cost to build? See page 134 to order complete cost estimate to build this house in your area!

LIVING RM. 12⁴ x 15⁰
ALCOVE
FAMILY RM. 13⁴ x 15⁰ + ALCOVE
DINING RM. 11⁴ x 12⁰
CURIOS
STOR.
P'TRY
CABT.
BKS.
COOK TOP
D.W.
PDR. RM.
UP DN
DESK
KITCHEN 14⁰ x 15⁰
FOYER
SER. ENT.
CL.
OVEN
REF.
CL.
PORCH
CURB
GARAGE 19⁴ x 19⁸

Width 40'
Depth 54'

Design by
Home Planners

BED RM. 11⁸ x 10⁸
SLOPED CEILING
UPPER FAMILY RM.
MASTER BED RM. 12⁰ x 16⁰
CL.
LIN.
BATH
RAILING
CL.
RAILING DN
S.
WHIRLPOOL
W.I.C.
SHLVS
DRSG.
W.I.C.
BED RM. 12⁰ x 10⁰
VANITY
SHLVS

47

Design 3638

Square Footage: 2,861

L

PRIVACY WALL

SPA

PRIVATE PATIO

Width 93'-4"
Depth 66'-6"

ENTERTAINMENT PATIO

MASTER SUITE
17⁰ x 13¹⁰
17'-0" CLG

MASTER BATH

BEDRM
12⁶ x 10⁰
10'-0" CLS

KIT
11⁶ x 14⁸
10'-0" CLS

ISLAND
VEG SINK

PANTRY
OVN

BATH

MORNING RM
13⁰ x 16⁰
14'-0" CLS

FAMILY RM
18⁰ x 12⁶
VOL CLG

SUNKEN

WALK-IN CLOSET

OFFICE-DEN
12² x 12⁰

BEDRM
12⁶ x 10⁰
10'-7" CLS

WET BAR
HVAC
LINEN
LAUNDRY ROOM
UTILITY SINK
BROOM CLOSET
WH
BATH

ARCHED COLONNADE
ARCHED COLONNADE

FOYER
14'-0" CLG

DINING RM
11¹⁰ x 12⁰
12'-0" CLS

LIVING RM
14⁰ x 12¹⁰
14'-0" CLS

GARAGE
23¹⁰ x 21⁶

GUEST RM
12⁰ x 10²
10'-0" CLS

COVERED PORCH

Quote One®

Cost to build? See page 134
to order complete cost estimate
to build this house in your area!

■ Double columns and an arched entry create a grand entrance to this elegant one-story home. Inside, arched colonnades add grace and definition to the formal living and dining rooms as well as the family room. The master suite occupies a separate wing, providing a private retreat. Treat yourself to luxury in the master bath which includes a bumped-out whirlpool tub, a separate shower and twin vanities. An office/den located nearby easily converts to a nursery. A snack bar provides space for meals on-the-go and separates the island kitchen from the bay-windowed morning room. Three additional bedrooms—one a guest room with an adjacent bath—share two baths.

Design by
Home Planners

Width 76'-6"
Depth 77'-4"

Design by
Home Planners

Design 3661

Square Footage: 2,385

L

A graceful covered porch leads to an elegant foyer which in turn guides you into the spacious great room. Here, a warming fireplace, built-in shelves and an entertainment center wait to welcome. A large island kitchen offers a nearby breakfast nook and has convenient access to the bayed dining room. At the other end of the home, double doors lead into an office that, with a nearby full bath, can also double as a guest suite. Double doors also lead into the luxurious master suite. Complete with a large walk-in closet, a sumptuous bath and a sitting room with access to a private patio/garden area, this suite provides lots of room to relax. Two secondary bedrooms, separated from the master for privacy, share a full bath. One bedroom has access to a private patio.

QUOTE ONE®

Cost to build? See page 134
to order complete cost estimate
to build this house in your area!

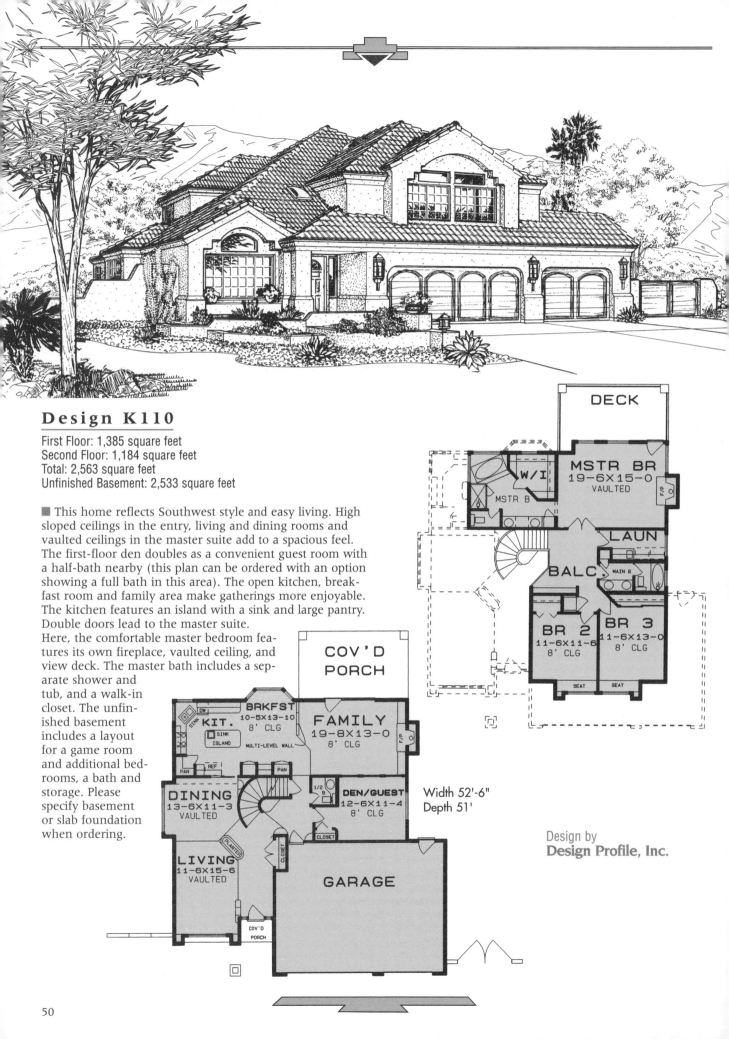

Design K110

First Floor: 1,385 square feet
Second Floor: 1,184 square feet
Total: 2,563 square feet
Unfinished Basement: 2,533 square feet

■ This home reflects Southwest style and easy living. High sloped ceilings in the entry, living and dining rooms and vaulted ceilings in the master suite add to a spacious feel. The first-floor den doubles as a convenient guest room with a half-bath nearby (this plan can be ordered with an option showing a full bath in this area). The open kitchen, breakfast room and family area make gatherings more enjoyable. The kitchen features an island with a sink and large pantry. Double doors lead to the master suite. Here, the comfortable master bedroom features its own fireplace, vaulted ceiling, and view deck. The master bath includes a separate shower and tub, and a walk-in closet. The unfinished basement includes a layout for a game room and additional bedrooms, a bath and storage. Please specify basement or slab foundation when ordering.

Width 52'-6"
Depth 51'

Design by
Design Profile, Inc.

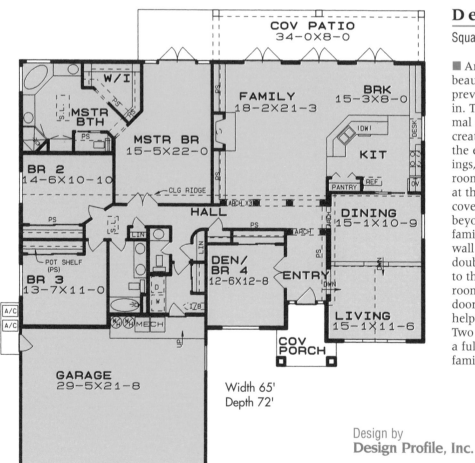

COV PATIO
34-0X8-0

FAMILY
18-2X21-3

BRK
15-3X8-0

MSTR
BTH

W/I

KIT

MSTR BR
15-5X22-0

BR 2
14-6X10-10

PANTRY   REF

DINING
15-1X10-9

CLG RIDGE

HALL

DEN/
BR 4
12-6X12-8

POT SHELF
(PS)

BR 3
13-7X11-0

LIN

ENTRY

A/C

A/C

MECH

LIVING
15-1X11-6

GARAGE
29-5X21-8

COV
PORCH

Width 65'
Depth 72'

Design K103

Square Footage: 2,708

■ An elegant exterior, graced by a beautiful arch and fine detailing, is a preview for the wonderful layout within. The separation of formal and informal areas of this Southwestern design creates casually elegant spaces. From the entry hall, with its arched openings, there is a view through the family room to the wall of glass French doors at the rear. These doors overlook the covered patio and the rear yard beyond. The colonnade of arches at the family room opens it up to a gallery wall near the fourth bedroom which doubles as a study. Double doors lead to the comfortable master suite with room for a sitting area near the French doors. A skylight in the master bath helps to complete the feel of luxury. Two nearby secondary bedrooms share a full hall bath and easily accommodate family and friends.

Design by
Design Profile, Inc.

Design 3641

Square Footage: 2,945

 L

■ A variety of hipped-roof planes with highly textured tiles cap this western hacienda. The stucco exterior wall surfaces are broken by effective window and door treatment. Fourteen-foot ceilings, columns, archways and a planter highlight a spacious and open-planned interior. Formal living and dining rooms flank the foyer. Straight ahead is the family's great room which functions well with the outdoor entertainment lanai. This plan features children's sleeping facilities which are located at opposite ends of the plan from those of the parents. The master bedroom is large and has its own outdoor living area complete with a fireplace and a spa.

Width 85'-10"
Depth 78'-5"

Design by
Home Planners

Quote One®

Cost to build? See page 134
to order complete cost estimate
to build this house in your area!

Design 3640

Square Footage: 2,612

L

BEDRM
12⁰ x 12⁴
9'-0" CLG

BEDRM
10⁴ x 13⁴
9'-0" CLG

BEDRM
10⁴ x 12⁰
9'-0" CLG

KIT
10⁰ x 14⁴
9'-0" CLG

FAMILY RM
19⁰ x 17¹⁰
9'-0" CLG

MASTER BEDRM
14⁸ x 14⁸
COFFERED CLG

MASTER BATH

SHOWER

GARDEN TUB

WALK-IN CLOSET

LINEN

STORAGE

COVERED PATIO

COVERED PATIO

COVERED PATIO

BATH

LIN

LAUNDRY

PDR RM

BG STORAGE

DINING
13⁶ x 10⁸
COFFERED CLG

FOYER

MEDIA/ OFFICE
14⁸ x 14⁸
9'-0" CLG

COVERED PORCH

GARAGE
21⁰ x 23⁶

Width 93'-7"
Depth 74'-10"

QUOTE ONE®
Cost to build? See page 134
to order complete cost estimate
to build this house in your area!

Design by
Home Planners

■ Spanish architecture meets modern livability in this fine one-story home. High rooflines and a columned entry add a sense of grand proportions, though the total square footage of the home is under 2,700 square feet. The unique floor plan makes it easy to live in. The family room holds court at the hub of the plan and features a corner fireplace and covered patio access. A media room or home office offers a more secluded space just across the foyer from the formal dining room. The master bedroom is split away from family bedrooms and features a walk-in closet fit for the largest wardrobes and a master bath with corner garden tub and separate shower. The island kitchen has eating space and access to a private dining porch. Family bedrooms share a full bath on the left side of the home. A two-car garage connects to the plan via a convenient laundry room.

Design 3311

Main Level: 2,662 square feet
Lower Level: 1,548 square feet
Total: 4,210 square feet

L D

■ Here's a hillside haven for family living with plenty of room to entertain in style. Enter the main level from a dramatic columned portico that leads to a large entry hall. The gathering room, graced by a fireplace and sliding glass doors to the rear deck, is straight back and adjoins a formal dining area. A true gourmet kitchen with plenty of room for casual eating and conversation is nearby. The abundantly appointed master suite on this level is complemented by a luxurious bath complete with His and Hers walk-in closets, a whirlpool tub in a bumped-out bay and a separate shower. Note the media room to the front of the house. On the lower level are two more bedrooms—each with access to the rear terrace, a full bath, a large activity area with fireplace and a convenient summer kitchen.

Design by
Home Planners

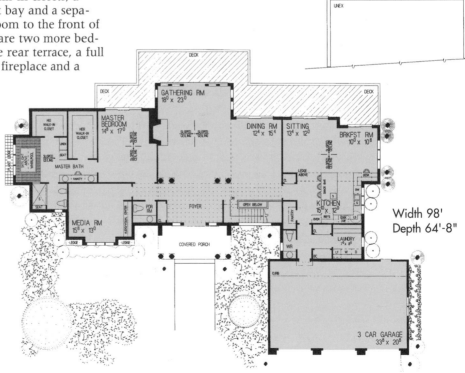

Width 98'
Depth 64'-8"

Quote One®

Cost to build? See page 134
to order complete cost estimate
to build this house in your area!

Design 8678

Square Footage: 3,091

■ With elegantly formal columns standing at attention around the entryway, this design starts off as impressive and only gets better. Inside, ceiling detail in the foyer and the formal dining room immediately reinforces the graceful qualities of this beautiful home. A large and airy living room awaits to accommodate any entertaining you might have in mind, while the spacious family room encourages more casual encounters with a warming fireplace and access to the covered patio. An angled kitchen is nearby and offers a sunny breakfast room for early morning risers. Three secondary bedrooms accommodate both family and friends, while a lavish master bedroom suite promises pampering for the fortunate homeowner.

Design by
**Home Design
Services, Inc.**

Pool

planter   planter

closet

Bedroom 3
volume ceiling
12⁰ · 12⁰

Bath

Master
Bath

planter

Covered
Patio

plant
shelf

summer
kitchen

Bedroom 4
volume ceiling
12⁰ · 12⁰

Family Room
volume ceiling
17⁶ · 29⁰

Master
Bedroom
volume ceiling
15⁵ · 19⁹

fireplace

Living Room
volume ceiling
14⁴ · 20⁰

Breakfast
volume ceiling

linen

w.i.c.

ac

w
d

ref

Utility

Kitchen

dw

Dining
14⁰ · 14⁰

Bath

mg
o
pantry

ac

Foyer

Bedroom 2
volume ceiling
13⁴ · 12⁰

wh

3 Car
Garage

planter   Entry   planter

Width 62'
Depth 83'-8"

Design 9578

Square Footage: 2,225

■ To complement its elegant exterior, inside, this home exemplifies clever floor patterning. Casual living takes off in the kitchen, nook and family room. A fireplace here will warm gatherings, while the many windows will fill the area with lots of natural sunlight. A formal dining room is nearby, as are a den with a double-door entry and a formal living room. A through-fireplace graces this space and creates a cozy atmosphere. In the deluxe master bedroom suite, a garden tub, a large walk-in closet and dual lavatories accommodate the owners. Two secondary bedrooms share a hall bath, also with dual lavatories. A laundry room connects the two-car garage.

QUOTE ONE®

Cost to build? See page 134 to order complete cost estimate to build this house in your area!

Design by
Alan Mascord
Design Associates, Inc.

MASTER
12/8 X 15/6
(10'-4" CLG.)

NOOK
11/0 X 11/6

BR 2
11/6 X 11/2
(9' CLG.)

FAMILY
15/0 X 18/0
(10'-4" CLG.)

11/0 X 11/2

DINING
16/2 X 10/8
(10'-4" CLG.)

BR 3
10/4 X 12/0
(9' CLG.)

(14'-1" CLG.)

DEN
10/6 X 12/0
(10'-4" CLG.)

GARAGE
19/4 X 20/8

LIVING
13/0 X 14/6
(15'-4" CLG.)

Width 45'
Depth 73'

Design by
Home Planners

TERRACE

COVERED PORCH

GATHERING RM.
16⁸ x 19⁴

MASTER BEDROOM
13⁰ x 13⁸

VANITY

DRSG. RM.

BATH

DINING RM.
12⁸ x 11⁰

WALK-IN CLOSET

SLOPED CEILING

8'-0" FLAT CEILING

BATH

TERRACE

BRKFST. RM.
10⁰ x 10⁸

OVENS

PASS THRU

REF'G

PTRY

DN

CL.

LIN.

CL.

SNACK BAR

KITCHEN
13⁸ x 10⁸

SLOPED CEILING

OPEN

DESK

B.C.

CL.

DW.

L.S.

FOYER

CL.

BEDROOM
10⁸ x 11⁴

BEDROOM
11⁴ x 11⁴

W.R.

MUD RM.

W.

PORCH

PLANT LEDGE

SLOPED CEILING

SLOPED CEILING

GARAGE
21⁴ x 21⁴

CURB

PLANT LEDGE

Width 66'
Depth 62'

Design 2912

Square Footage: 1,864

■ This contemporary design with smart Spanish styling incorporates careful zoning by room functions with lifestyle comfort. All three bedrooms, including a master bedroom suite, are isolated at one end of the home. Entry to a breakfast room and kitchen is possible through a mud room off the garage. That's good news for people carrying groceries from car to kitchen or slipping off muddy shoes during inclement weather. The efficient kitchen includes a snack bar and convenient cooktop with multiple access to the breakfast room, side foyer, and pass-through to the great room. There's also a nearby formal dining room. A large rear gathering room features a sloped ceiling and a fireplace. A covered porch extends living potential.

Quote One®

Cost to build? See page 134
to order complete cost estimate
to build this house in your area!

Design 3665

Square Footage: 2,678

L

■ A gracefully covered porch leads
to an elegant foyer which in turn
guides you into the spacious great
room. A warming fireplace waits to
welcome, while built-in shelves and
an entertainment center reinforce a
feeling of relaxation. A large island
kitchen offers a nearby breakfast
nook and has convienient access to
the bayed dining room. At the other
end of the home is an office which,
with a nearby full bath, can also
double as a great guest suite. The
luxurious master suite is complete
with a large walk-in closet, a sumptuous bath and a sitting room with
access to a private patio/garden area,
and is sure to please. Two secondary
bedrooms, separated from the master for privacy, share a full bath.
One bedroom has access to a private
patio. A third bedroom, also good
for a guest suite, is separated from
the main traffic flow and located
near the garage.

Design by
Home Planners

Width 76'-6"
Depth 77'-4"

Cost to build? See page 134
to order complete cost estimate
to build this house in your area!

SOUTHWEST TRANSITIONS

Design 9740

Square Footage: 1,838

■ Arched windows and a dramatic arched entry enhance this exciting Southwestern home. The expansive great room, highlighted by a cathedral ceiling and a fireplace, offers direct access to the rear patio and the formal dining room—a winning combination for both formal and informal get-togethers. An efficient U-shaped kitchen provides plenty of counter space and easily serves both the dining room and the great room. Sunlight floods the master bedroom and affords views of the rear grounds with its wall of windows. The master bath invites relaxation with its soothing corner tub and separate shower. Two secondary bedrooms (one serves as an optional den) share an adjacent bath.

Design by
**Donald A. Gardner,
Architects, Inc.**

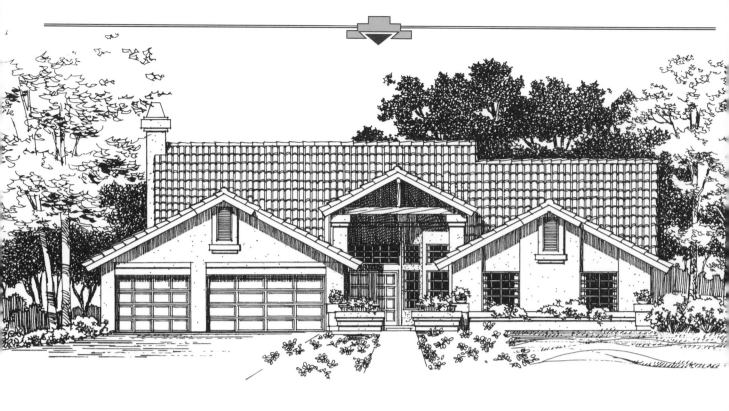

Design 3423

Square Footage: 2,577

■ This spacious Southwestern home will be a pleasure to come home to. Immediately off the foyer are the dining room and step-down living room with bay window. The highlight of the four-bedroom sleeping area is the master suite with porch access and a whirlpool for soaking away the day's tensions. The informal living area features an enormous family room with a fireplace and a bay-windowed kitchen with a breakfast room and a snack bar pass-through to the family room. A three-car garage fulfills the family needs.

Quote One®

Cost to build? See page 134 to order complete cost estimate to build this house in your area!

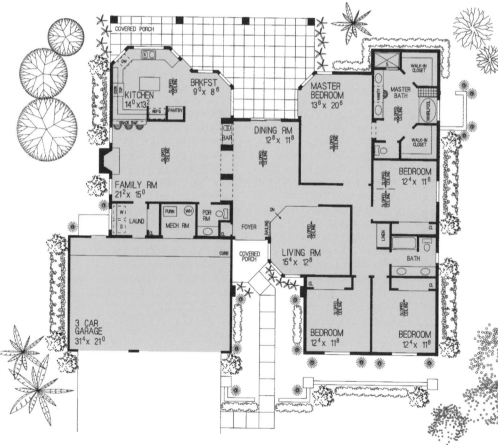

Width 72'
Depth 57'-4"

Design by
Home Planners

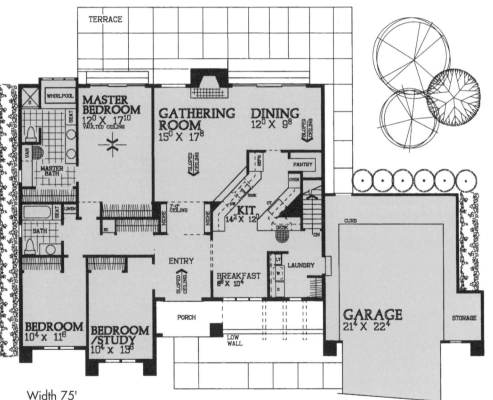

TERRACE

MASTER
BEDROOM
12⁰ X 17¹⁰
VAULTED CEILING

WHIRLPOOL

SEAT

VAN

MASTER
BATH

SEAT LINEN

BATH

NICHE
7'-0" CEILING

NICHE

GATHERING
ROOM
15⁰ X 17⁸
SLOPED CEILING

DINING
12⁰ X 9⁸
SLOPED CEILING

PANTRY

OVEN

KIT
14² X 12⁰

SINK

DESK

ENTRY
SLOPED CEILING

BEDROOM
10⁴ x 11⁶

BEDROOM
/STUDY
10⁴ x 13⁶

PORCH

LOW
WALL

BREAKFAST
8⁰ X 10⁴

LAUNDRY

CURB

GARAGE
21⁴ X 22⁴

STORAGE

Width 75'
Depth 47'-5"

Design 3480

Square Footage: 1,845

L **D**

Design by
Home Planners

Cost to build? See page 134
to order complete cost estimate
to build this house in your area!

■ Beyond the grand entry, a comfortable gathering room, with a central fireplace, shares sweeping, open spaces with the dining room. An efficiently patterned kitchen makes use of a large, walk-in pantry and a breakfast room. A snack bar offers a third mealtime eating option. Nearby, a full laundry room rounds out the modern livability of this utilitarian area. Away from the hustle and bustle of the day, three bedrooms provide ample sleeping accommodations for the whole family. Two secondary bedrooms each enjoy full proportions and the convenience of a nearby bath. In the master bedroom, look for double closets and a pampering bath with double lavs, a vanity and a whirlpool bath.

Cost to build? See page 134 to order complete cost estimate to build this house in your area!

Design 2948

Square Footage: 1,830

■ Styled for Southwest living, this home is a good choice in many regions. Among its many highlights are a gathering room/dining room combination that includes a fireplace, snackbar pass-through, and sliding glass doors to the rear terrace. The kitchen is uniquely shaped and sports a huge walk-in pantry plus breakfast room with windows on the front covered porch. Bedrooms include a master suite with sloped ceiling, access to the rear terrace, and a private bath. Two additional bedrooms share a full bath. One of these bedrooms makes a fine study and features built-in shelves for books as well as a built-in cabinet.

Width 75'
Depth 43'-5"

Design by
Home Planners

Design by
Home Planners

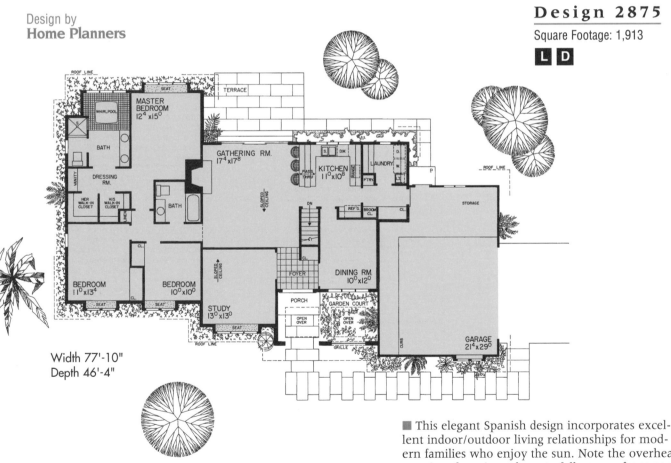

Width 77'-10"
Depth 46'-4"

QUOTE ONE®

Cost to build? See page 134
to order complete cost estimate
to build this house in your area!

■ This elegant Spanish design incorporates excellent indoor/outdoor living relationships for modern families who enjoy the sun. Note the overhead openings for rain and sun to fall upon a front garden, while a twin-arched entry leads to the front porch and foyer. Inside, the floor plan features a modern kitchen with pass-through to a large gathering room with fireplace. Other features include a dining room, laundry room, a study off the foyer, plus three bedrooms including a master bedroom with its own whirlpool.

Design 3440

Square Footage: 2,290

L

■ There's plenty of room to accommodate family growth in this three-, or optional four-bedroom home. The expansive gathering room welcomes family and guests with a through-fireplace to the dining room, an audio/visual center and a door to the outside. The kitchen includes a wide pantry, a snack bar and a separate eating area. Included in the master suite: two walk-in closets, a separate shower, a whirlpool tub and seat, dual vanities and linen storage. Three secondary bedrooms—or make one a cozy den—share a full bath with dual vanities. A three-car garage easily accommodates the family vehicles.

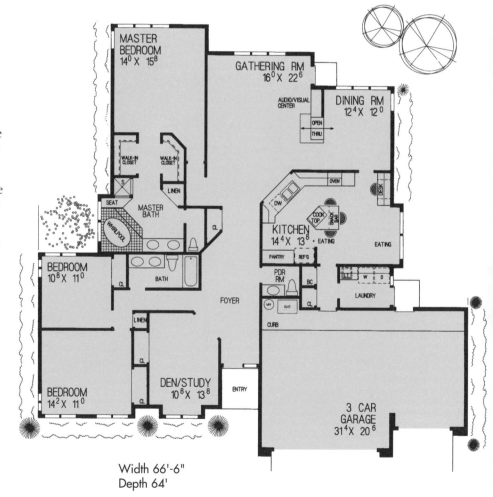

MASTER
BEDROOM
14⁰ X 15⁸

GATHERING RM
16⁰ X 22⁶

DINING RM
12⁴ X 12⁰

AUDIO/VISUAL
CENTER

OPEN
THRU

WALK-IN
CLOSET

WALK-IN
CLOSET

LINEN

SEAT

MASTER
BATH

WHIRLPOOL

OVEN

DW

COOK
TOP

KITCHEN
14⁴ X 13⁸

DESK

EATING

EATING

PANTRY

REF'G

CL

BATH

BEDROOM
10⁸ X 11⁰

CL

PDR
RM'

BC

W D

LAUNDRY

FOYER

MH

A/C

CL

LINEN

CURB

BEDROOM
14² X 11⁰

CL

DEN/STUDY
10⁸ X 13⁸

CL

ENTRY

3 CAR
GARAGE
31⁴ X 20⁶

Width 66'-6"
Depth 64'

Design by
Home Planners

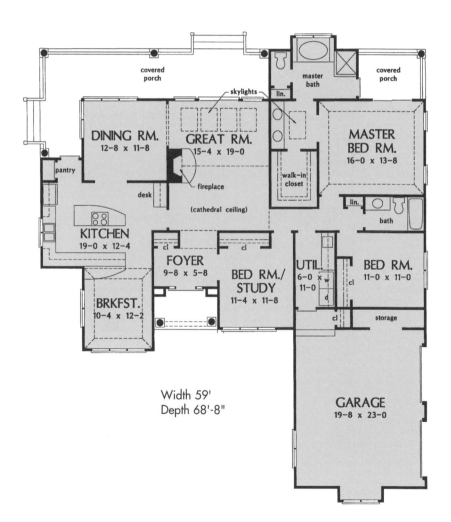

covered porch

DINING RM.
12-8 x 11-8

skylights

GREAT RM.
15-4 x 19-0

master bath

lin.

covered porch

MASTER BED RM.
16-0 x 13-8

pantry

desk

fireplace

(cathedral ceiling)

walk-in closet

lin.

bath

KITCHEN
19-0 x 12-4

cl

cl

FOYER
9-8 x 5-8

BED RM./
STUDY
11-4 x 11-8

UTIL.
6-0 x
11-0

w
d

cl

BED RM.
11-0 x 11-0

BRKFST.
10-4 x 12-2

cl

storage

Width 59'
Depth 68'-8"

GARAGE
19-8 x 23-0

Design 9737

Square Footage: 1,929

■ Make the most of warmer climes in this striking three-bedroom home. A grand entry gives way to a great room with skylights and a fireplace. A cathedral ceiling furthers the open feeling in this room. A large dining room surveys views on two sides. Adjacent, the kitchen will delight with its large island work space and abundance of counter and cabinet space. Facing the front, the breakfast room offers ample space along with elegant ceiling detail. Three bedrooms—or two with a study—make up the sleeping quarters of this plan. In the master bedroom, large proportions include a private bath with dual lavs, a walk-in closet and a bumped-out garden tub. A secluded covered porch provides the opportunity for outdoor enjoyment. Please specify crawlspace or slab foundation when ordering.

Design by
**Donald A. Gardner,
Architects, Inc.**

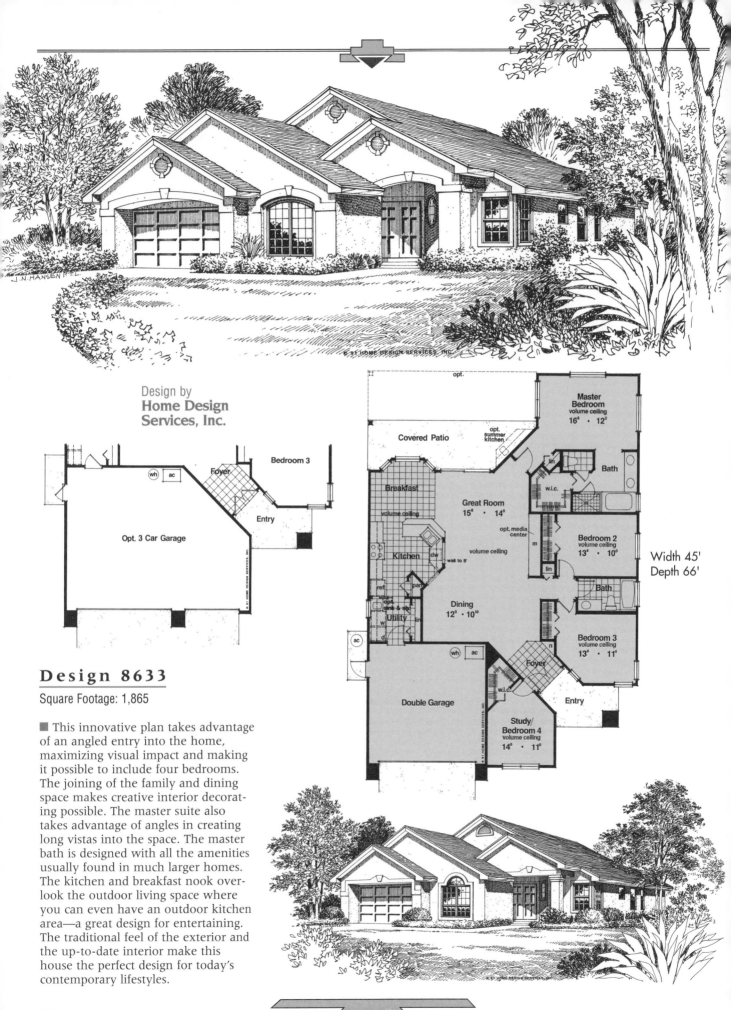

Design by
**Home Design
Services, Inc.**

Opt. 3 Car Garage

Foyer
Bedroom 3
Entry

Covered Patio
opt.
opt. summer kitchen

Master Bedroom
volume ceiling
16⁸ · 12⁰

Bath

Breakfast
volume ceiling

lin
w.i.c.

Great Room
15⁸ · 14⁰

opt. media center

Bedroom 2
volume ceiling
13⁴ · 10⁰

Kitchen
dw
wall to 8'

volume ceiling

lin

Bath

ref
par.

opt.
sink & stb.

Dining
12⁰ · 10¹⁰

Bedroom 3
volume ceiling
13⁴ · 11⁴

Utility
lin

ac

Foyer
n

Width 45'
Depth 66'

ac
wh
ac

Double Garage

w.i.c.

Entry

Study/
Bedroom 4
volume ceiling
14⁰ · 11⁰

Design 8633

Square Footage: 1,865

■ This innovative plan takes advantage
of an angled entry into the home,
maximizing visual impact and making
it possible to include four bedrooms.
The joining of the family and dining
space makes creative interior decorat-
ing possible. The master suite also
takes advantage of angles in creating
long vistas into the space. The master
bath is designed with all the amenities
usually found in much larger homes.
The kitchen and breakfast nook overlook the outdoor living space where
you can even have an outdoor kitchen
area—a great design for entertaining.
The traditional feel of the exterior and
the up-to-date interior make this
house the perfect design for today's
contemporary lifestyles.

© 91 HOME DESIGN SERVICES, INC.

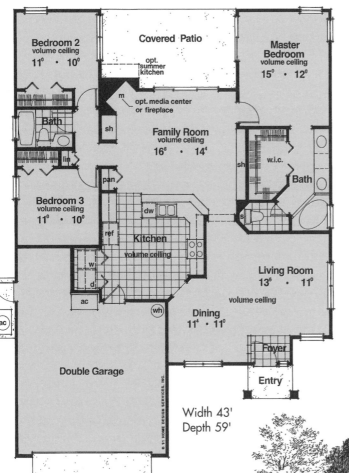

Bedroom 2
volume ceiling
11⁰ · 10⁰

Covered Patio

opt. summer kitchen

Master Bedroom
volume ceiling
15⁰ · 12⁰

Bath

sh

m

opt. media center or fireplace

Family Room
volume ceiling
16⁸ · 14⁴

sh

w.i.c.

Bath

pan

Bedroom 3
volume ceiling
11⁰ · 10⁰

dw

ref

Kitchen
volume ceiling

s

w

d

ac

wh

Living Room
13⁶ · 11⁰
volume ceiling

Dining
11⁴ · 11⁰

Foyer

Entry

ac

Double Garage

Width 43'
Depth 59'

Design by
Home Design Services, Inc.

Design 8630

Square Footage: 1,550

■ This plan has it all! A formal living and dining area as you enter is just the beginning. The eat-in country kitchen overlooking the family room and outdoor living space makes this plan the ultimate family house. The home is designed for adults, however, because it pampers with a master suite featuring a vaulted ceiling and oversized master bath with sitting area. The private toilet room adds a special touch. Even though the look of this home is traditional, special details such as the media space in the family room make it very contemporary. Plans for this home include a choice of two exterior elevations.

Design HPT464001

First Floor: 1,618 square feet
Second Floor: 1,212 square feet
Total: 2,830 square feet
Bonus Room: 376 square feet

■ The strong lines, arched windows and a stucco finish complement the facade and enhance this attractive transitional design. The two-story foyer, with its angled stair, opens to the dramatically vaulted living room on one side and the den with French doors on the other. An efficient L-shaped island kitchen works well with the formal dining room to the left and a sunny nook to the right. A bayed family room with a warming hearth completes this floor. A spacious master bedroom provides luxury with a spa tub, walk-in closet, dual vanities and separate shower. Two family bedrooms and a vaulted bonus room share a full hall bath.

Design by
Alan Mascord Design Associates, Inc.

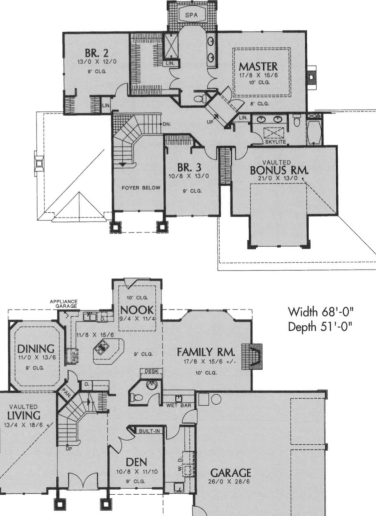

Width 68'-0"
Depth 51'-0"

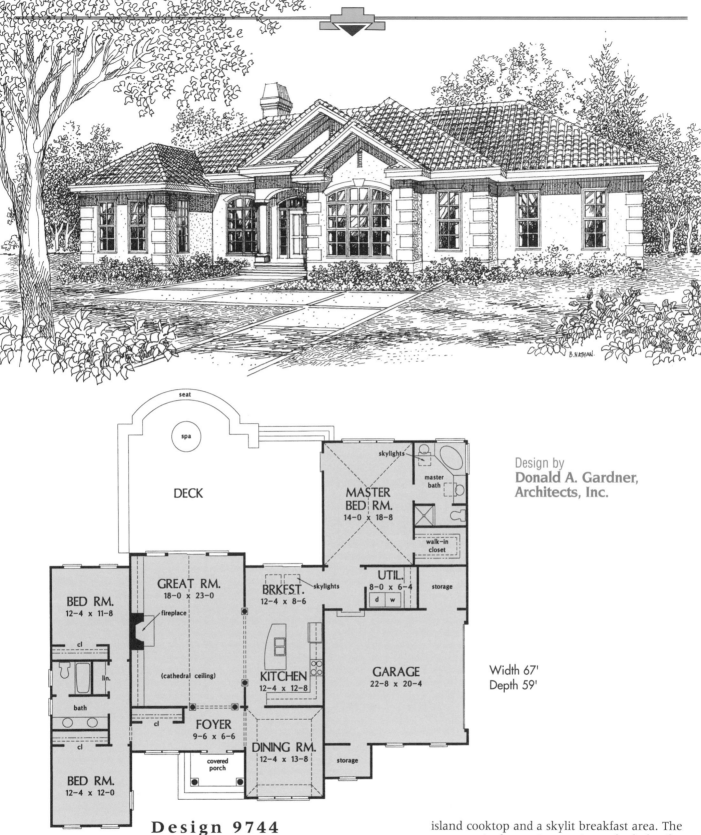

Design by
Donald A. Gardner,
Architects, Inc.

Width 67'
Depth 59'

Design 9744

Square Footage: 2,090

■ This exciting Southwestern design is enhanced by the use of arched windows and an inviting arched entrance. The large foyer opens to a massive great room with a fireplace and built-in cabinets. The kitchen features an island cooktop and a skylit breakfast area. The master suite has an impressive cathedral ceiling and a walk-in closet as well as a luxurious bath that boasts separate vanities, a corner whirlpool tub and a separate shower. Two additional bedrooms are located at the opposite end of the home for privacy and share a full bath. Please specify crawlspace or slab foundation when ordering.

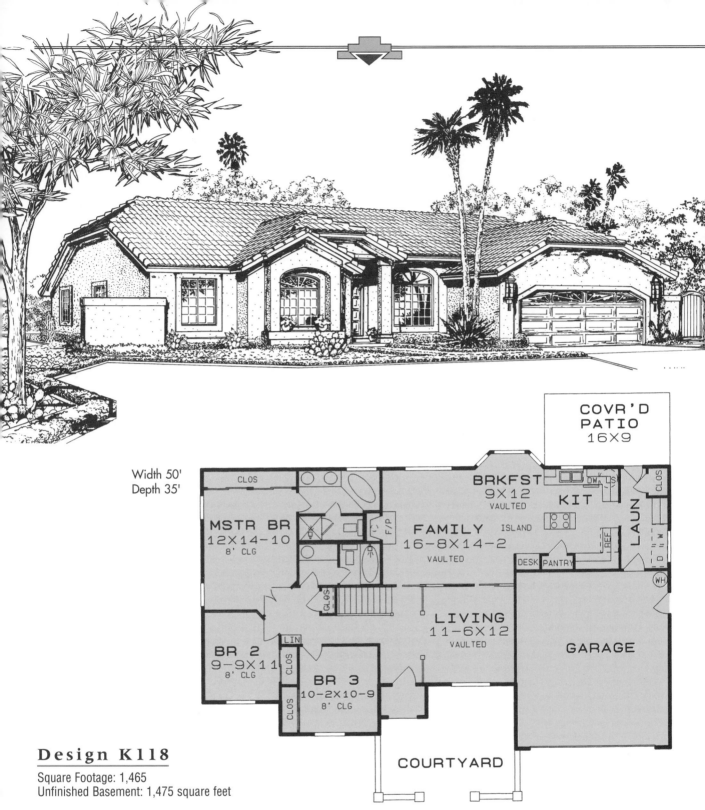

Width 50'
Depth 35'

COVR'D PATIO 16X9

CLOS

BRKFST 9X12 VAULTED

KIT

DW

LS

CLOS

LAUN

MSTR BR 12X14-10 8' CLG

F/P

FAMILY 16-8X14-2 VAULTED

ISLAND

REF

DESK PANTRY

WH

CLOS

LIVING 11-6X12 VAULTED

GARAGE

LIN

CLOS

BR 2 9-9X11 8' CLG

BR 3 10-2X10-9 8' CLG

CLOS

COURTYARD

Design K118

Square Footage: 1,465
Unfinished Basement: 1,475 square feet

■ This compact home offers lots of family living for the size. The open plan features double doors between the formal and family areas to allow flexible use or privacy as the need arises. Removing the wall between these areas opens the plan up to a 26'x17' great room. Easy access to the rear yard is gained from the breakfast and laundry rooms. The open kitchen features a center island with a range and a built-in planning desk. The unfinished basement includes room for three more bedrooms, a large game room, a bath and lots of extra storage. Please specify basement or slab foundation when ordering.

Design by
Design Profile, Inc.

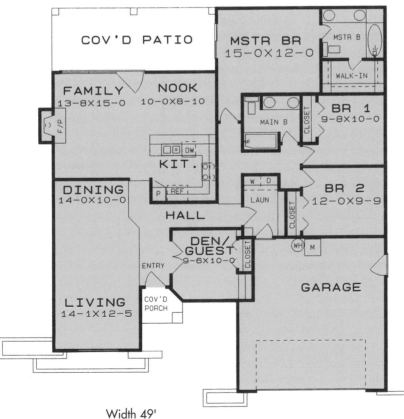

COV'D PATIO

FAMILY
13-8X15-0

NOOK
10-0X8-10

KIT.

DINING
14-0X10-0

HALL

LIVING
14-1X12-5

ENTRY

COV'D
PORCH

DEN/
GUEST
9-6X10-0

CLOSET

MSTR BR
15-0X12-0

MSTR B

WALK-IN

MAIN B

CLOSET

BR 1
9-8X10-0

W   D

LAUN

CLOSET

BR 2
12-0X9-9

WH   M

GARAGE

F/P

P   REF

DW

Width 49'
Depth 49'

Design K119

Square Footage: 1,743
Optional Basement: 1,743 square feet

■ Attractive rooflines and an elegant column at the entryway give this design plenty of curb appeal. Though designed as a three-bedroom, it has a den/guest room that can be converted into a fourth bedroom if needed. This flexible space can also serve as a home office with its double doors facing into the formal living and dining areas. The open family-kitchen area is warmed by a fireplace and features a wall of glass leading to the large covered patio at the rear. Two secondary bedrooms share a hall bath while the deluxe master suite offers a private bath and a walk-in closet. This plan is also available with a basement which adds plenty of expansion space. Please specify basement or slab foundation when ordering.

Design by
Design Profile, Inc.

Design 3375

Square Footage: 1,378

L D

■ Prepare for warmer climes with this two- or three-bedroom home. A covered porch with columns leads to the interior where a breakfast room sits to the left and a media room (or use this room as a bedroom) sits to the right. Directly ahead, in the living room, a fireplace and a sloped ceiling lend definition. The dining room is open to this area and features sliding glass doors to a rear terrace. In the kitchen, a U-shape assures efficiency. Two bedrooms include a master suite with a private bath, a box-bay window and a walk-in closet.

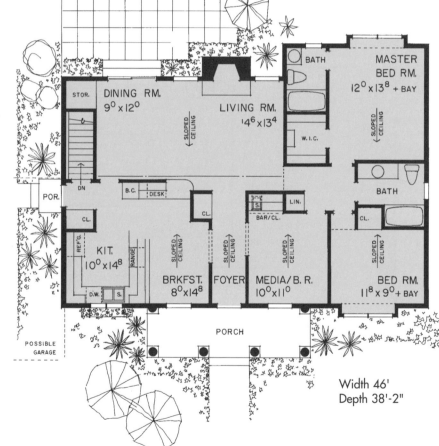

Width 46'
Depth 38'-2"

QUOTE ONE®
Cost to build? See page 134
to order complete cost estimate
to build this house in your area!

Design by
Home Planners

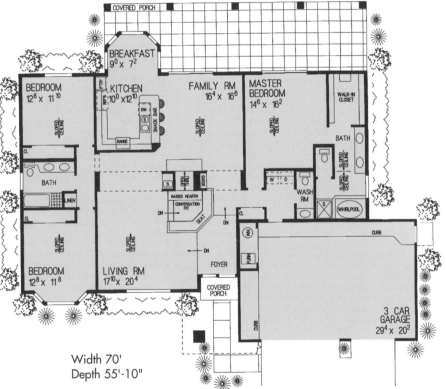

COVERED PORCH

BREAKFAST
9⁰ x 7²

BEDROOM
12⁸ x 11¹⁰

KITCHEN
10⁰ x 12¹⁰

FAMILY RM
16⁴ x 16⁶

MASTER BEDROOM
14⁶ x 16²

WALK-IN CLOSET

SLOPED CEILING

SNACK BAR

DW

RANGE

SLOPED CEILING

SLOPED CEILING

BATH

BATH

LINEN

RAISED HEARTH

CONVERSATION PIT

SEAT

WASH RM

SLOPED CEILING

WHIRLPOOL

BEDROOM
12⁸ x 11⁸

LIVING RM
17¹⁰ x 20⁴

SLOPED CEILING

FOYER

COVERED PORCH

CURB

3 CAR GARAGE
29⁴ x 20²

CURB

Width 70'
Depth 55'-10"

Design by
Home Planners

Design 3421

Square Footage: 2,145

L

QUOTE ONE®

Cost to build? See page 134
to order complete cost estimate
to build this house in your area!

■ Split-bedroom planning makes the most of a one-story design. In this case the master suite is on the opposite side of the house from two family bedrooms. Gourmets can rejoice at the abundant work space in the U-shaped kitchen and will appreciate the natural light afforded by the large bay window in the breakfast room. A formal living room has a sunken conversation area with a cozy fireplace as its focus. The rear covered porch can be reached through sliding glass doors in the family room.

QUOTE ONE®

Cost to build? See page 134
to order complete cost estimate
to build this house in your area!

Design 3422

Square Footage: 1,932

L

■ An enclosed entry garden greets visitors to this charming Southwestern home. Inside, the foyer is flanked by formal and informal living areas—a living room and dining room to the right and a cozy study to the left. To the rear, a large family room with a fireplace, a bay-windowed breakfast room and an open kitchen have access to a covered porch, and overlook the back yard. The three-bedroom sleeping area includes a master suite with a spacious bath that features a whirlpool tub.

Design by
Home Planners

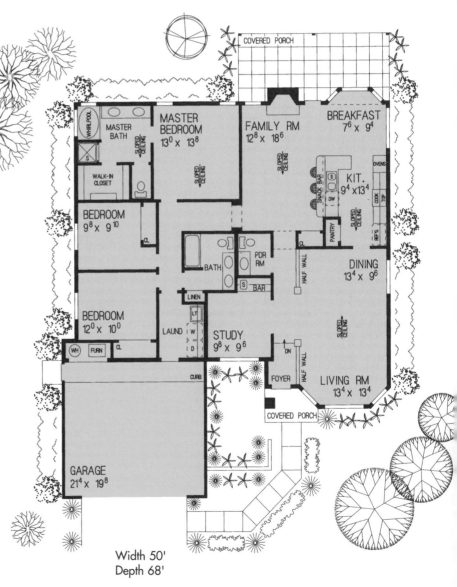

Width 50'
Depth 68'

Design by
Home Planners

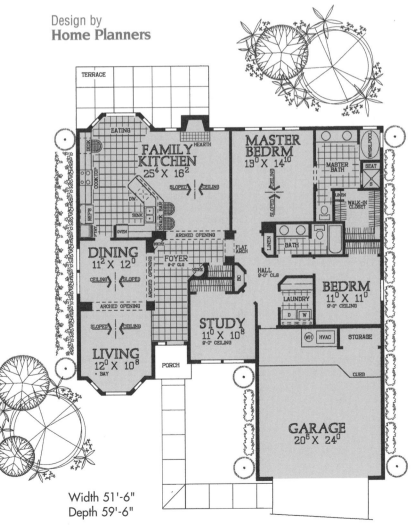

TERRACE

EATING

FAMILY KITCHEN
25⁴ X 16²

DESK

REF.

PTY.

COOK TOP

DW.

SNACK BAR

SINK

OVEN

SLOPED ← CEILING

HEARTH

MASTER BEDRM
13⁰ X 14¹⁰

SLOPED → CEILING

MASTER BATH

WHIRLPOOL

SEAT

LINEN

WALK-IN CLOSET

ARCHED OPENING

NICHE

FLAT ARCH

LINEN

BATH

DINING
11² X 12⁰

CEILING ↓ ↑ SLOPED

FOYER
9'-0" CLG

ARCHED OPENING

NICHE

R.C.

HALL
9'-0" CLG

BEDRM
11⁰ X 11⁰
9'-0" CEILING

ARCHED OPENING

LAUNDRY

D | W

ARCHED OPENING

SLOPED ← CEILING

STUDY
11⁰ X 10⁸
9'-0" CEILING

WH HVAC

STORAGE

LIVING
12⁰ X 10⁸
• BAY

PORCH

CURB

GARAGE
20⁸ X 24⁰

Width 51'-6"
Depth 59'-6"

QUOTE ONE®

Cost to build? See page 134
to order complete cost estimate
to build this house in your area!

Design 3478

Square Footage: 1,898

L

■ Small but smart describes this one-story
plan that provides a maximum of livability in a compact plan. The living and dining rooms project a sense of space with
sloped ceilings, flat arches and plenty of
space above for plants, decorative pots or
family treasures. The kitchen shares space
with the bayed breakfast nook, providing
accessibility to the back yard through sliding glass doors. The adjacent family room
enjoys a fireplace, creating a living area
ideal for informal gatherings. Sleeping
quarters consist of the master suite, a secondary bedroom and a study that may be
used as a third bedroom if needed. The
master bedroom boasts a whirlpool tub
and a large walk-in closet.

Design by
Home Planners

Design 3569

Square Footage: 1,981

L D

■ A graceful entry opens this impressive one-story design; the foyer introduces an open gathering room/dining room combination. A front-facing study could easily convert into a bedroom for guests—a full bath is directly accessible from the rear of the room. In the kitchen, such features as an island cooktop and a built-in desk add to livability. A corner bedroom takes advantage of front and side views. The master bedroom accesses the rear terrace and also sports a bath with dual lavatories and a whirlpool. Other special features of the house include multi-pane windows, a warming fireplace, a cozy covered dining porch and a two-car garage.

QUOTE ONE®

Cost to build? See page 134
to order complete cost estimate
to build this house in your area!

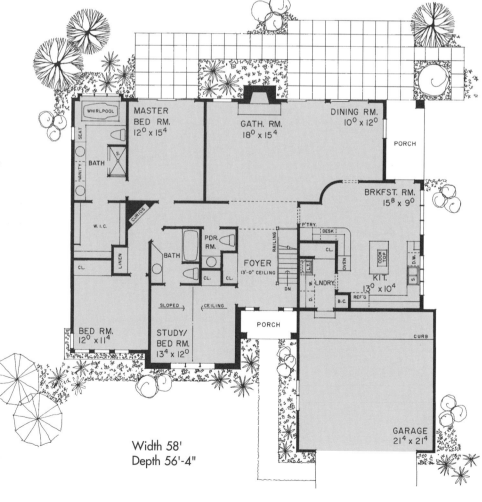

Width 58'
Depth 56'-4"

Design by
Home Planners

GUEST
BEDROOM
11⁰ x 10⁶

COVERED PORCH

MASTER
BEDROOM
13⁰ x 17⁶

MASTER
BATH

WHIRLPOOL

WALK-IN
CLOSET

BRKFST RM
9⁴ x 9⁰

BEDROOM
11⁴ x 9⁶

KITCHEN
12⁰ x 11⁸

BEDROOM
10⁸ x 10⁶

BATH

BATH

FAMILY RM
17⁶ x 14⁰

BEDROOM
11⁴ x 10⁴

MECH RM

PANTRY

LAUNDRY
D W

DINING RM
11⁶ x 12⁸

FOYER

LIVING RM
16⁰ x 13⁴

3 CAR
GARAGE
28² x 20⁸ + STORAGE

STORAGE

COVERED
PORCH

Width 70'
Depth 63'

Design 3411

Square Footage: 2,441

L

■ You'll love the entry to this Southwestern home—it creates a dramatic first impression and leads beautifully to the formal living and dining rooms. Beyond, look for an open family room and breakfast room in the same proximity as the kitchen. Sliding glass doors here open to a back yard patio. Take your choice of four bedrooms or five, depending on how you wish to use the optional room. The huge master suite is located to the rear of the plan for privacy. This quiet retreat features passage to the covered porch and a master bath filled with amenities that include a relaxing whirlpool tub and a huge walk-in closet.

QUOTE ONE®

Cost to build? See page 134
to order complete cost estimate
to build this house in your area!

Design 3419

Square Footage: 1,965

L

■ This attractive, multi-gabled exterior houses a compact, livable interior. The entry foyer effectively routes traffic to all areas: left to the family room and kitchen, straight back to the dining room and living room, and right to the four-bedroom sleeping area. The spacious family room provides an informal gathering space while the living and dining rooms are perfect for formal occasions. The highlight of the sleeping area is the master bedroom with its whirlpool tub, walk-in closet and view of the back yard.

Width 56'
Depth 56'

Design by
Home Planners

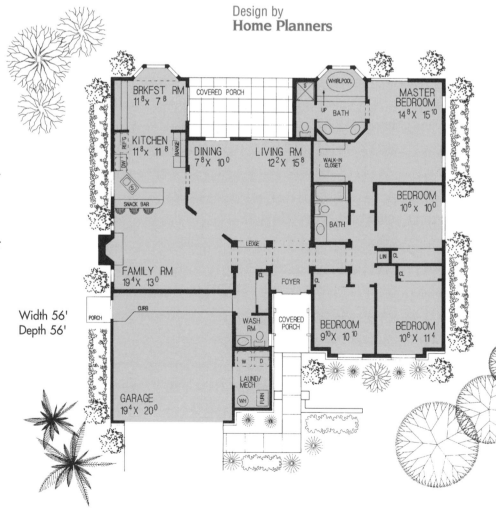

Cost to build? See page 134
to order complete cost estimate
to build this house in your area!

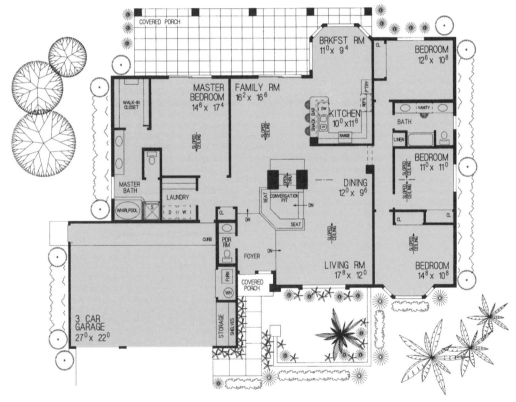

COVERED PORCH

BRKFST RM
11⁰ x 9⁴

BEDROOM
12⁸ x 10⁸

WALK-IN
CLOSET

MASTER
BEDROOM
14⁶ x 17⁴

FAMILY RM
16² x 16⁶

KITCHEN
10⁰ x 11⁶

P'TRY

SNACK BAR

SLOPED CEILING

SLOPED CEILING

VANITY

BATH

MASTER
BATH

LAUNDRY

RANGE

DINING
12⁰ x 9⁶

LINEN

BEDROOM
11⁰ x 11⁰

SLOPED CEILING

WHIRLPOOL

CONVERSATION PIT

SEAT

SEAT

DN

CL

SLOPED CEILING

CURB

PDR RM

DN

FOYER

DN

LIVING RM
17⁸ x 12⁰

SLOPED CEILING

BEDROOM
14⁸ x 10⁸

FURN

COVERED
PORCH

WH

STORAGE

SHELVES

3 CAR
GARAGE
27⁰ x 22⁰

Width 72'
Depth 60'-6"

Design by
Home Planners

Design 3430

Square Footage: 2,394

L

■ This dramatic design bene-
fits from open planning. The
centerpiece of the living area
is a sunken conversation pit
which shares a through-fireplace with the family room.
The living room and dining
room share space beneath a
sloped ceiling. The open
kitchen features a snack bar
and breakfast room and conveniently serves all living
areas. Split zoning in the
sleeping area places the private master suite to the left of
the plan and three more bedrooms, including one with a
bay window, to the right.

QUOTE ONE®

Cost to build? See page 134
to order complete cost estimate
to build this house in your area!

Design by
Home Planners

Width 74'
Depth 66'-10"

Design 2950

Square Footage: 2,559

■ A natural desert dweller, this stucco, tile-roofed beauty is equally comfortable in any clime. Inside, there's a well-planned design. Common living areas—gathering room, formal dining room, and breakfast room—are offset by a quiet study that could be used as a bedroom or guest room. A master suite features two walk-in closets, a double vanity and a whirlpool spa. The two-car garage provides a service entrance; close by is an adequate laundry area and a pantry. A lovely hearth warms the gathering room and complements the snack-bar eating area.

QUOTE ONE®

Cost to build? See page 134
to order complete cost estimate
to build this house in your area!

Floor Plan

Width 64'
Depth 52'

QUOTE ONE®

Cost to build? See page 134
to order complete cost estimate
to build this house in your area!

Design by
Home Planners

First Floor Plan Labels

BAY

BREAKFAST
10⁶ X 10⁴ + BAY

COVERED PATIO

KITCHEN
13⁰ X 11⁰

SNACK BAR

S / DW

FAMILY RM
17⁰ X 13⁶

SLOPED CEILING

PANTRY

NICHE

REF / G

DINING RM
11⁶ X 9⁸

OVEN

BATH

ART GALLERY

RAILING

SLOPED CEILING

MECH

LAUNDRY

D

W

UP

NICHE

LIVING RM
14⁰ X 14⁰

FOYER

GARAGE
19¹⁰ X 17⁴

CURB

GAME RM
11⁰ X 19⁰

BEDROOM
10¹⁰ X 11⁴

CL

COVERED PORCH

Design 3447

First Floor: 1,861 square feet
Second Floor: 1,039 square feet
Total: 2,900 square feet

L **D**

■ This classic stucco home is designed to make the most of family entertainment. The first floor includes a game room, a front-facing bedroom that would be perfect for out-of-town guests and a large family room with a fireplace and access to a rear covered patio. The spacious, angled kitchen features a snack bar and a corner pantry. It is located conveniently close to both the bay-windowed breakfast room and the combination dining room and living room. The elegant staircase provides a perfect focal point for family portraits or your favorite artist. The master bedroom features a private deck, two closets and a corner whirlpool tub. Two additional bedrooms share a galley-style bath.

Second Floor Plan Labels

ROOF

RAILING

DECK

MASTER BEDROOM
13⁴ X 16⁶

S

WHIRLPOOL

MASTER BATH

OPEN TO FAMILY RM BELOW

SLOPED CEILING

SLOPED CEILING

SLOPED CEILING

WALK-IN CLOSET

OPEN TO LIVING RM BELOW

SLOPED CEILING

ART GALLERY

RAILING

RAILING

DN

BATH

LINEN

WH

CL

OPEN TO FOYER BELOW

ATTIC ACCESS

BEDROOM
11¹⁰ X 10⁴

BEDROOM
11⁰ X 12⁸

ATTIC STORAGE

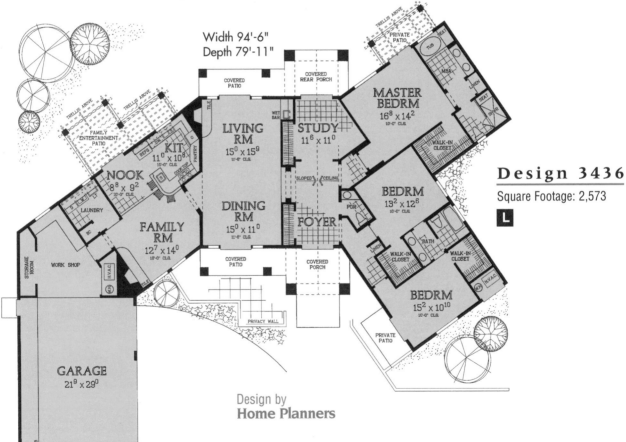

Width 94'-6"
Depth 79'-11"

COVERED PATIO

COVERED REAR PORCH

PRIVATE PATIO
TRELLIS ABOVE

TUB
MBA
SEAT
LINEN
SEAT
SHWR

MASTER BEDRM
16⁸ x 14²
10'-0" CLG.

WALK-IN CLOSET

Design 3436

Square Footage: 2,573

L

FAMILY ENTERTAINMENT PATIO
TRELLIS ABOVE

WET BAR

LIVING RM
15⁰ x 15⁹
11'-6" CLG.

STUDY
11⁶ x 11⁰

KIT.
11⁰ x 10⁸
10'-0" CLG.
REF.
COOK TOP
PANTRY

NOOK
8⁸ x 9²
10'-0" CLG.

SLOPED CEILING

BEDRM
13² x 12⁶
10'-0" CLG.

LAUNDRY

DINING RM
15⁰ x 11⁰
11'-6" CLG.

FOYER

PDR

BATH
LINEN
LINEN

FAMILY RM
12⁷ x 14⁰
10'-0" CLG.

COVERED PATIO

COVERED PORCH

WALK-IN CLOSET

WALK-IN CLOSET

STORAGE ROOM

WORK SHOP

HVAC

PRIVACY WALL

BEDRM
15² x 10¹⁰
10'-0" CLG.

HVAC

GARAGE
21⁸ x 29⁰

CURB

PRIVATE PATIO

Design by
Home Planners

■ This dashing Spanish home, with its captivating front courtyard, presents a delightful introduction to the inside living spaces. These excel with a central living room/dining room combination. A wet bar here makes entertaining easy. In the kitchen, a huge pantry and interesting angles are sure to please the house gourmet. A breakfast nook with a corner fireplace further enhances this area. The master bedroom makes room for a private bath with a whirlpool tub and dual lavatories; a walk-in closet adds to the amenities found here. Two additional bedrooms make use of a Hollywood bath. Each bedroom is highlighted by a spacious walk-in closet.

Design by
Home Planners

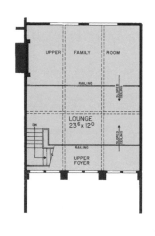

Width 104'-6"
Depth 58'-4"

Design 2670

Square Footage: 3,058
Lounge: 279 square feet

L

■ A centrally located interior atrium is just one of the interesting features of this Spanish design. The atrium has a built-in seat and will bring light to its adjacent rooms: living room, dining room and breakfast room. Beyond the foyer, sunken one step, is a tiled reception hall that includes a powder room. This area leads to the sleeping wing and up one step to the family room with its raised-hearth fireplace. Overlooking the family room is a railed lounge which can be used for various activities. Sleeping areas include a master suite and three family bedrooms.

QUOTE ONE®

Cost to build? See page 134
to order complete cost estimate
to build this house in your area!

© The Sater Group, Inc.

■ The wonderfully balanced exterior of this Floridian design offers triple columns with circle-top windows at the covered entry. Inside, the formal living and dining rooms face the rear, with large glass doors providing excellent views to the veranda and beyond. The kitchen, nook and leisure room unite to provide a grand space for casual gatherings. The living room includes an optional wet bar. Bedrooms are planned for maximum privacy. The secondary bedrooms share a full bath; a separate lanai is available to Bedroom 2. The master wing includes a study that can serve as a reading room, a home office or a guest bedroom. It is conveniently located near the entry and has a powder room and a coat closet. The master suite includes a bayed area and a master bath with a garden tub, a large shower and His and Hers walk-in closets.

Design by
**The Sater
Design Collection**

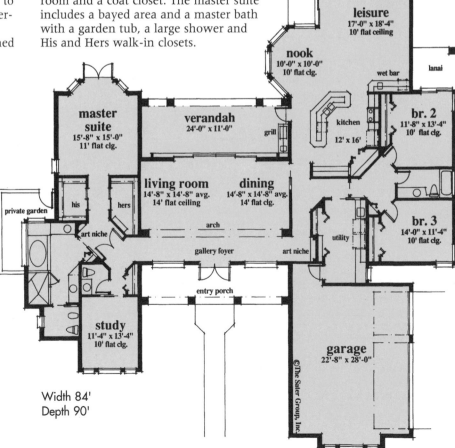

Design 6663

Square Footage: 2,978

Width 84'
Depth 90'

This home, as shown in the photograph, may differ from the actual blueprints.
For more detailed information, please check the floor plans carefully.

Photo by Home Design Services

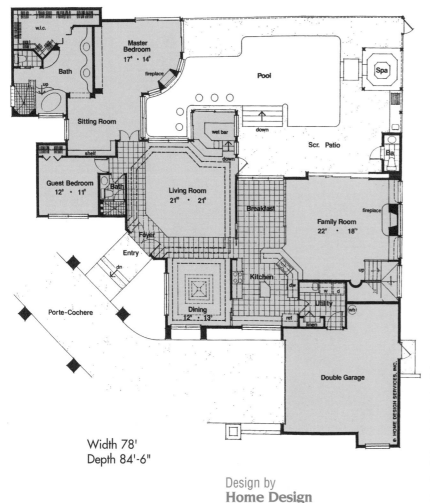

Width 78'
Depth 84'-6"

Design by
**Home Design
Services, Inc.**

Design 8625

First Floor: 2,669 square feet
Second Floor: 621 square feet
Total: 3,290 square feet

■ Varying rooflines, arches and corner quoins adorn the facade of this magnificent home. A porte cochere creates a stunning prelude to the double-door entry. A wet bar serves the sunken living room and overlooks the pool area. The dining room has a tray ceiling and is located near the gourmet kitchen with prep island and angled counter. A guest room opens off the living room. The generous family room, warmed by a fireplace, opens to the screened patio. The master bedroom has a sitting room and fireplace set into an angled wall. Its luxurious bath includes a step-up tub. Upstairs, two bedrooms share the oversized balcony and nearby observation room.

Design 2843

Upper Level: 1,861 square feet
Lower Level: 1,181 square feet
Total: 3,042 square feet

Design by
Home Planners

L

■ Bi-level living will be enjoyed to its fullest in this handsome Spanish styled design. This one has been planned for efficiency, both upstairs and down. The upper level contains the living room and formal dining room; they share a fireplace, and each leads to a comfy deck out back. In addition, the kitchen and breakfast area are centers of attention; the latter has a wonderful, oversized pantry. Zoned to the left of the entry are three bedrooms (two if you make one a study). The lower level is a potpourri of space: family room, lounge with raised-hearth fireplace, large laundry room (note the boxed-bay window), another bedroom, full bath and plenty of storage in the garage.

Width 54'
Depth 40'-4"

QUOTE ONE®
Cost to build? See page 134
to order complete cost estimate
to build this house in your area!

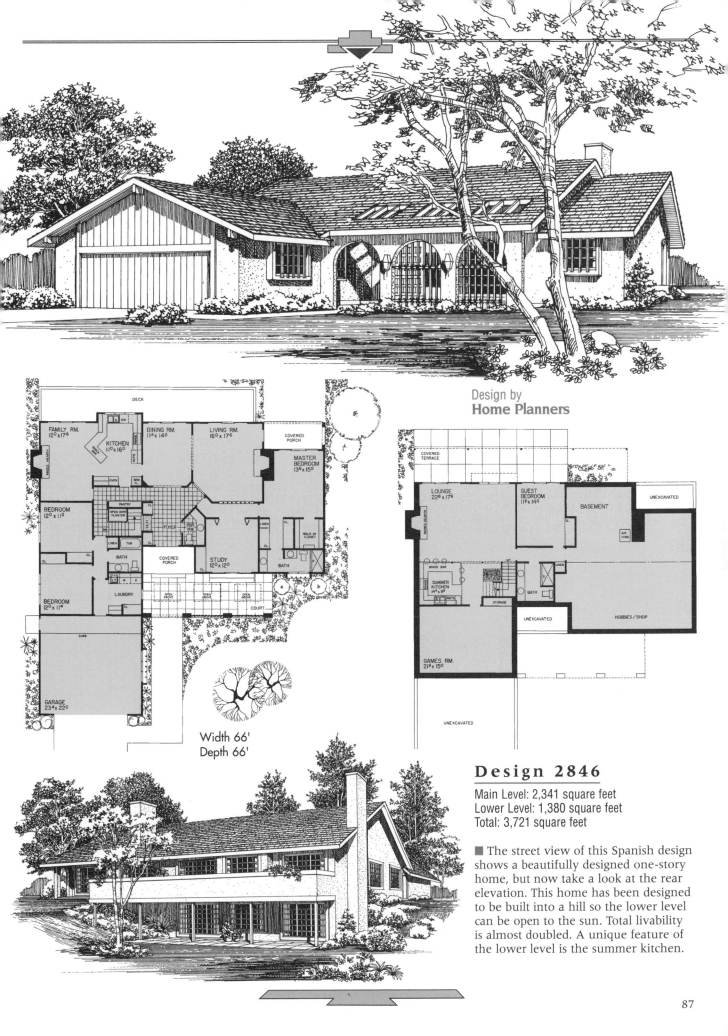

Design by
Home Planners

Width 66'
Depth 66'

Design 2846

Main Level: 2,341 square feet
Lower Level: 1,380 square feet
Total: 3,721 square feet

■ The street view of this Spanish design shows a beautifully designed one-story home, but now take a look at the rear elevation. This home has been designed to be built into a hill so the lower level can be open to the sun. Total livability is almost doubled. A unique feature of the lower level is the summer kitchen.

Design 3463

First Floor: 1,163 square feet
Second Floor: 1,077 square feet
Total: 2,240 square feet

L

■ Fine family living takes off in this grand two-story plan. The tiled foyer leads to a stately living room with sliding glass doors to the back terrace and columns separating it from the dining room. Additional accents include a corner curios niche and access to a covered porch. For casual living, look no further than the family room/breakfast room combination. The kitchen supplies an island counter in the midst of its accommodating layout. On the second floor, the master bedroom offers a fireplace, access to a deck and a spoiling bath. A smart addition, the study niche in the hallway shares the outside deck. Two family bedrooms wrap up the sleeping facilities.

Design by
Home Planners

Width 42'
Depth 72'-8"

TERRACE

COVERED PATIO

FAMILY RM.
14¹⁰X14²

BRKFST.
KITCHEN
13⁶X19⁶

MASTER
BEDRM.
12⁰X16⁴

FIRE
PLACE

CAB'T.

SNACK BAR

OVEN

CK. TOP

REFG.

CL

LIN

W.I.C.

SHOWER

PWDR.
RM.

MASTER BATH

WHIRLPL.

LAUNDRY

W.
D.

DN

UP

OPEN

PTRY.

DK.

CL

FOYER

DINING
RM.
13²X11⁰

GARAGE
19⁴X19⁶

LIVING RM.
13²X16⁰

QUOTE ONE®

Cost to build? See page 134
to order complete cost estimate
to build this house in your area!

UPPER
MASTER
BEDRM.

TRAY CLG.

UPPER
FAMILY RM.

UPPER
BRKFST.

RAILG.

BATH

BEDRM.
10⁰X11⁸

RAILG.

DN

LINEN

CL

CL

BEDRM.
13⁴X11⁰

BEDRM.
12⁴X11⁸

W.I.C.

RAILING

UPPER
FOYER

UPPER
LIVING RM.

Design 3464

First Floor: 1,776 square feet
Second Floor: 876 square feet
Total: 2,652 square feet

L **D**

■ If you're looking for something a little different from the
rest, this dramatic home may end your search. A two-story
foyer introduces an open formal area consisting of a volume
living room and a dining room separated by columns. The
kitchen sits to the rear of the plan and shares space with the
breakfast room. Here, a curved wall adds interest—sliding
glass doors take you out to a covered porch and a connecting terrace. The family room enjoys access to this terrace
while maintaining great indoor livability with its see-
through fireplace and volume ceiling. Also on the first floor,
the master bedroom offers to its lucky occupants a pampering bath. The sleeping accommodations are complete with
three upstairs bedrooms.

Design by
Home Planners

Design 3475

Square Footage: 3,286

Design by
Home Planners

■ The colorful, tiled hipped roof with varying roof planes and wide overhangs sets off this Spanish design. Meanwhile, the sheltered front entrance is both dramatic and inviting with double doors opening to the central foyer. Here, a long plant shelf serves as a nice introduction. In the sunken living room, a curved, raised-hearth fireplace acts as a focal point. Double glass doors lead to a covered terrace. The U-shaped kitchen is efficient with its island work surface, breakfast bar, pantry and broom closet. An informal nook delights with its projecting bay and high ceiling. This generous, open area extends to include the family room and will cater to many of the family's informal living activities. Opposite the more formal living room is the separate dining room. Its expanse of glass looks out on the garden court. A major floor-planning feature of this design is found in the sleeping arrangements; notice the complete separation of the master suite from the secondary bedrooms.

QUOTE ONE®

Cost to build? See page 134
to order complete cost estimate
to build this house in your area!

Width 77'-4"
Depth 74'-8"

Design 3602/3603

Square Footage: 2,312/2,520

L

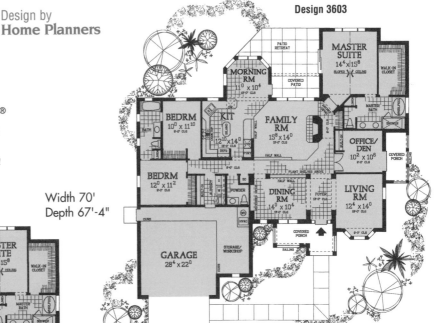

Design 3603

Design by
Home Planners

QUOTE ONE®

Cost to build? See page 134
to order complete cost estimate
to build this house in your area!

Width 70'
Depth 67'-4"

Design 3602

■ This lovely one-story home—with its two- and three-bed-room options- fits right into sunny regions. Its stucco exterior with easily accessed outdoor living areas makes it an all-time favorite. Inside, the floor plan accommodates empty-nester lifestyles. There is plenty of room for both formal and informal entertaining: living room, dining room, family room and morning room. An office/den with a private covered porch provides a quiet getaway for reflective thinking. Sleeping areas are split with the master bedroom and bath on one side and secondary sleeping quarters and a bath on the other. Other special features include a warming hearth in the family room and a grand rear deck. Please specify Design 3602 for the two-bedroom option and Design 3603 for the three-bedroom option.

Design 3631

Square Footage: 2,813

L

■ Symmetry reigns supreme on the exterior of this Spanish-style design. In the center is a portico with three arches that frame the entryway, while double turrets on either side feature large, multi-pane windows with circle-head tops. The floor plan allows for the open lifestyle so coveted in the Southwest. Flanking the foyer are the formal living room and formal dining room—each large enough for carefree entertaining. The rear of the home contains a wonderfully open area with the family room and U-shaped kitchen. A covered patio enhances casual living. To further pamper homeowners, the master suite offers walk-in closets, a private office with covered porch, an exercise area and access to a deck with spa tub. Family bedrooms (three of them!) share a full bath. One of the bedrooms has its own private porch.

Design by
Home Planners

Width 84'
Depth 77'

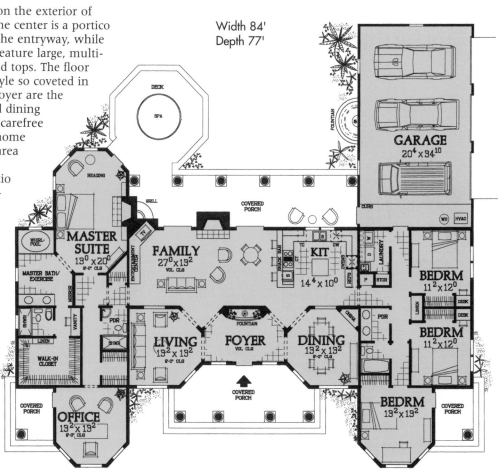

LIGHT-FILLED HOMES

J.W. HANSEN

© 91 HOME DESIGN SERVICES, INC.

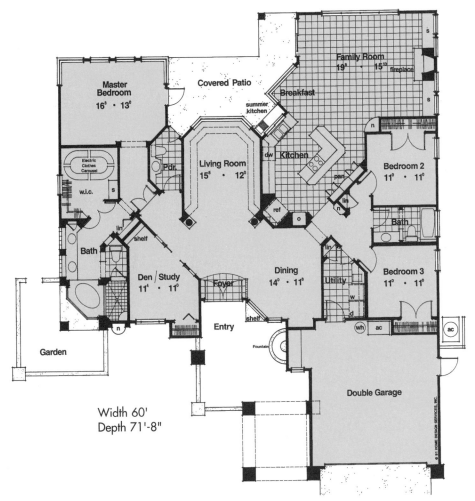

Master Bedroom 16⁰ · 13⁰

Covered Patio

Family Room 19⁸ · 15¹⁰ fireplace

Breakfast

summer kitchen

Electric Clothes Carousel

w.i.c.

Pdr.

Living Room 15⁵ · 12⁰

dw **Kitchen**

pan

ref

Bedroom 2 11⁰ · 11⁰

Bath

Bath

shelf

lin

Den / Study 11⁴ · 11⁰

Foyer

Dining 14⁰ · 11⁰

Utility

w d

Bedroom 3 11⁰ · 11⁰

shelf

Entry

wh ac

ac

Garden

Fountain

Double Garage

Width 60'
Depth 71'-8"

© 91 HOME DESIGN SERVICES, INC.

Design 8672

Square Footage: 2,397

■ Low-slung, hipped rooflines and an abundance of glass enhance the unique exterior of this fine one-story home. Inside, the use of soffits and tray ceilings heightens the distinctive style of the floor plan. To the left, double doors lead to the private master suite which is bathed in natural light—compliments of an abundant use of glass—and enjoys a garden setting from the corner tub. Convenient planning of the gourmet kitchen places everything at minimum distances. The kitchen serves the outdoor kitchen, breakfast nook and family room with equal ease. Completing the plan are two family bedrooms that share a full bath.

Design by
Home Design Services, Inc.

Design 8662

Square Footage: 2,005

■ A super floor plan makes this volume home that much more attractive. Inside you'll find a formal dining room—defined by columns—to the right and a living room—with an optional fireplace—to the left. Beyond this area is an expansive great room with a vaulted ceiling that opens to the kitchen and breakfast room. A covered patio in the back of the house enhances outdoor livability. Two secondary bedrooms complete the right side of the plan. Each features a volume ceiling, ample closet space and the use of a full hall bath with dual lavatories. The master bedroom enjoys its own bath with a whirlpool tub, separate shower, dual vanity and compartmented toilet.

Design by
**Home Design
Services, Inc.**

Design by
**Home Design
Services, Inc.**

Design 8683

First Floor: 2,254 square feet
Second Floor: 608 square feet
Total: 2,862 square feet

■ Indoor/outdoor relationships are enhanced by the beautiful courtyard that decorates the center of this home. A gallery provides views of the courtyard and leads to a kitchen featuring a center work island and an adjacent breakfast room offering easy access to the back yard. Combined with the family room, this space will be a favorite for informal gatherings. To the left, the gallery leads to the formal living room and master suite. The secluded master bedroom features a tray ceiling and double doors that lead to a covered patio. Retreat to the master bath, where a relaxing tub awaits to pamper and enjoy. The second floor contains a full bath shared by Bedroom 3 and 4 and a loft with its own balcony that provides flexible space for an additional bedroom.

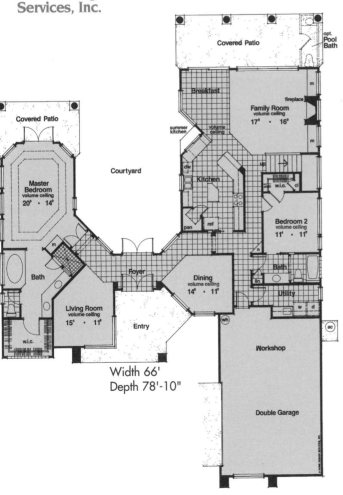

Width 66'
Depth 78'-10"

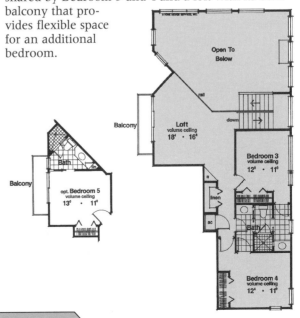

Design 8667

Square Footage: 2,258

■ Columns add the finishing touches to a home with a choice of facades. The double-door entry opens to the foyer with a front-to-back view. The adjacent vaulted living room has sliding glass doors to the covered patio. The kitchen is open to the living room, the formal dining room and the bayed nook. A bow window and a fireplace define the rear of the family room. The tray-ceilinged master bedroom features covered patio access, dual walk-in closets and a spa tub with spectacular window treatment. Two additional bedrooms share a full bath with a bumped-out bay window. A study adjacent to the master bedroom, with a full bath nearby, can be turned into a fourth bedroom if needed. The plan includes both elevations.

Design by
Home Design Services, Inc.

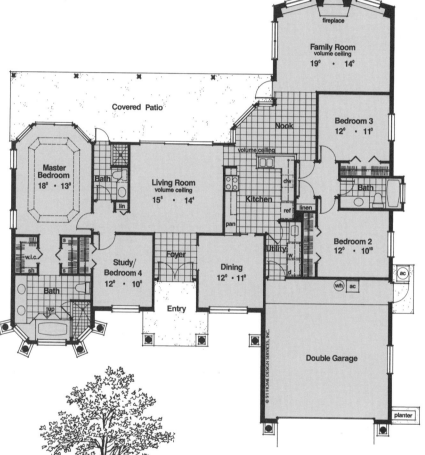

Covered Patio

Master Bedroom
18⁰ · 13⁰

Bath

lin

Living Room
volume ceiling
15⁰ · 14⁴

Family Room
volume ceiling
19⁰ · 14⁰

fireplace

Nook

volume ceiling

Bedroom 3
12⁰ · 11⁰

dw

Kitchen

Bath

ref

linen

w.l.c.

sh

Bath

up

Study/ Bedroom 4
12⁰ · 10⁰

Foyer

Dining
12⁰ · 11⁰

Utility

w

d

Bedroom 2
12⁰ · 10⁰

pan

wh

ac

ac

Entry

Double Garage

planter

Width 66'
Depth 73'-4"

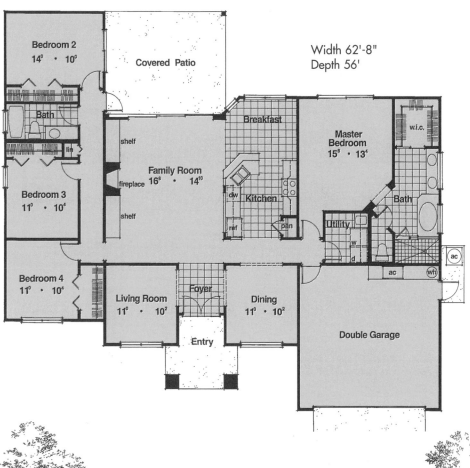

Bedroom 2
14⁰ · 10⁰

Covered Patio

Width 62'-8"
Depth 56'

Bath

Breakfast

Master
Bedroom
15⁸ · 13⁴

w.i.c.

shelf

Family Room
16⁸ · 14¹⁰

fireplace

shelf

dw

Kitchen

Bath

ref

pan

Bedroom 3
11⁰ · 10⁴

Utility

w

d

Bedroom 4
11⁰ · 10⁴

Living Room
11⁰ · 10²

Foyer

Dining
11⁰ · 10²

ac

ac

wh

Entry

Double Garage

Design 8636

Square Footage: 2,010

■ Not only does this house look exciting from the outside, with its contemporary use of glass, but upon entering this home, the excitement continues. The classic split living room and dining room sets this house apart from the rest. The family room, breakfast nook and kitchen all share the views to the rear yard. The efficient placement of the bedrooms creates privacy for family members. The master suite is ample, with a wonderful bath featuring a lounging tub, shower, private toilet room, double vanities and generous walk-in closet. Plans for this home include a choice of two exterior elevations.

Design by
**Home Design
Services, Inc.**

Design 8673

Square Footage: 2,398

■ This three-bedroom home also has
a three-car garage. The casual areas of
the home remain open to each other
for lots of family time. To the front of
the plan, a den/study easily converts
to a bedroom, should guests come to
visit. Nearby, a formal dining room
includes a tray ceiling and columns.
The living room accesses a covered
patio. The master bedroom's bath also
provides passage to this area—perfect
accommodations for a pool. Two family bedrooms enjoy a built-in desk
and a roomy bath that also has outdoor access. The large family room
and nook area is easily served by the
kitchen which features a pantry and
island work surface. Off the covered
patio, a summer kitchen facilitates
added pool-time fun.

Design by
**Home Design
Services, Inc.**

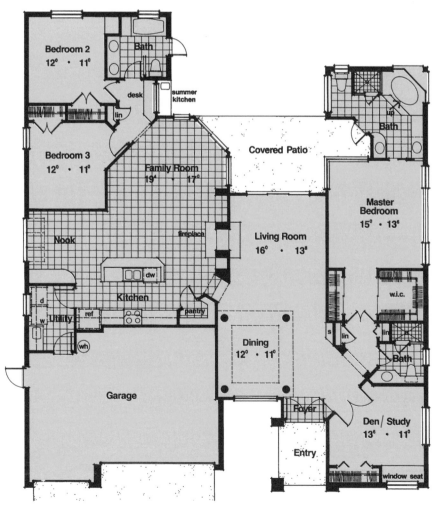

Width 57'-6"
Depth 66'

Bedroom 4
13⁰ • 11⁰

Family Room
18⁸ • 14⁰

fireplace

Covered Patio

Design 8669

Square Footage: 2,287

Breakfast

Bath

lin

lin
dw

Kitchen

rf

pantry

Living Room
16⁰ • 14⁰

Master
Bedroom
18⁰ • 15⁰

Bedroom 3
13⁰ • 11⁰

Utility

w

ac   wh

d   lin

Dining
12⁸ • 10⁸

Foyer

Pdr.

w.i.c.

w.i.c.

Bath

up

lin

Double Garage

Width 63'-4"
Depth 62'-4"

Entry

Den /
Bedroom 2
12⁰ • 11⁸

■ This sunny home offers a wealth of livability in less than 2,300 square feet. The covered entry gives way to living and dining rooms. The kitchen is well equipped with a pantry and a breakfast room. The family room is a few steps away and delights with a fireplace. Two family bedrooms reside on this side of the plan. The master bedroom offers large proportions and an expansive bath with dual walk-in closets, a double-bowl lavatory, a whirlpool tub, a separate shower and a compartmented toilet. A den is located off the entry and can also serve as another bedroom.

Design 8649

Square Footage: 2,691

■ Italianate lines add finesse to the formal facade of this home. Strong symmetry, a soaring portico and gentle rooflines are the prized hallmarks of a relaxed, yet formal design. A stepped fourteen-foot ceiling highlights the foyer. To the right, columns and a stepped twelve-foot ceiling offset the dining room. A plant soffit heralds the living room which also has a twelve-foot ceiling. An angled cooktop counter adds flair to the kitchen, which also has a desk and walk-in pantry and serves the breakfast nook. A corner fireplace and a patio enhance the family room. An arch opens the entry to the lavish master suite. Two additional bedrooms come with separate entries to a full bath.

Width 78'-6"
Depth 73'-10"

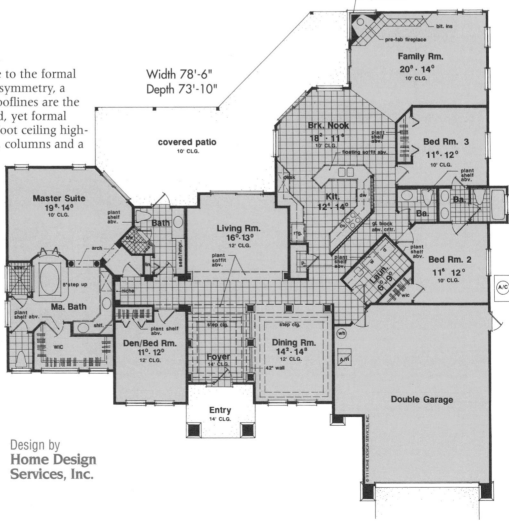

Design by
**Home Design
Services, Inc.**

Width 65'
Depth 60'

covered patio

Master Suite
16⁰ x 14⁰

wet bar

fireplace

Sitting Area
16⁰ x 12⁰

Ma. Ba.

wic

ba.

Bed Rm. 4
10⁰ x 11⁰

Living Rm.
13⁹ x 12⁰

Foyer

Entry

Family Rm.
18⁰ x 24⁰

Brk. Nook
12⁸ x 12⁴

Kit.
13⁰ x 12⁴

Dining Rm.
12⁰ x 14⁰

ba.

Bed Rm. 2
11⁰ x 13⁰

lin.

Bed Rm. 3
12⁸ x 12⁰

La.

A/C

wh

2 Car Garage
19⁸ x 26⁸

Design 8676

Square Footage: 2,726

■ Designed for a larger family, this four-bedroom one-story holds many features that will appeal to savvy tastes. The covered entry opens through double doors to a central foyer that gives access to the living areas of the home: formal living and dining rooms and an open family room with a fireplace. The kitchen includes an island work area and a glass-enclosed breakfast room that overlooks the rear covered patio. The right side of the home has two bedrooms that share a full bath and access to the rear patio. The left side holds the master suite, which contains a wet bar, a three sided fireplace, a sitting area and a compartmented bath with a separate tub and shower. Another smaller bedroom with nearby bath works well as a guest suite or nursery.

Design by
**Home Design
Services, Inc.**

Design 8604

Square Footage: 2,153

■ Sophistication and elegance are the bywords of this four-bedroom, two bath home. Among the many special features are a dramatic foyer, a column-encircled dining room, and twelve-foot ceilings. The kitchen is a true gourmet's delight and opens to a light-filled breakfast nook. The family room is enhanced by a barrel ceiling and a fireplace. Secondary bedrooms are separated from the master suite. Each contains a spacious closet; two contain corner windows. The master suite is luxurious with a walk-in closet, sliding glass doors to the rear porch and a bath with a double sink and a step-up tub.

Design by
**Home Design
Services, Inc.**

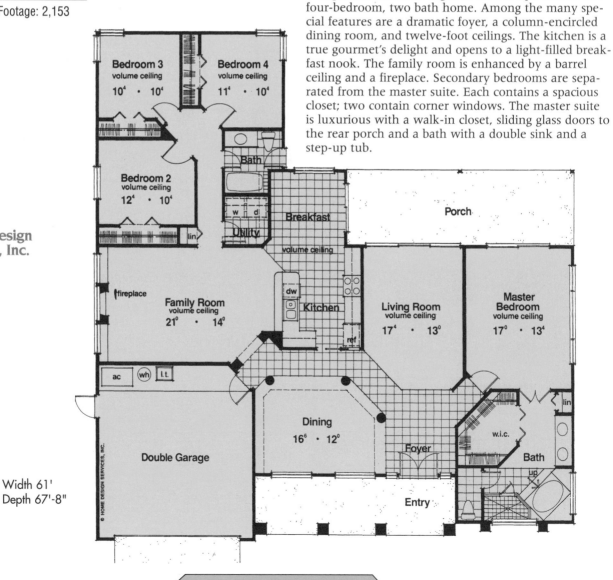

Width 61'
Depth 67'-8"

Design by
**Home Design
Services, Inc.**

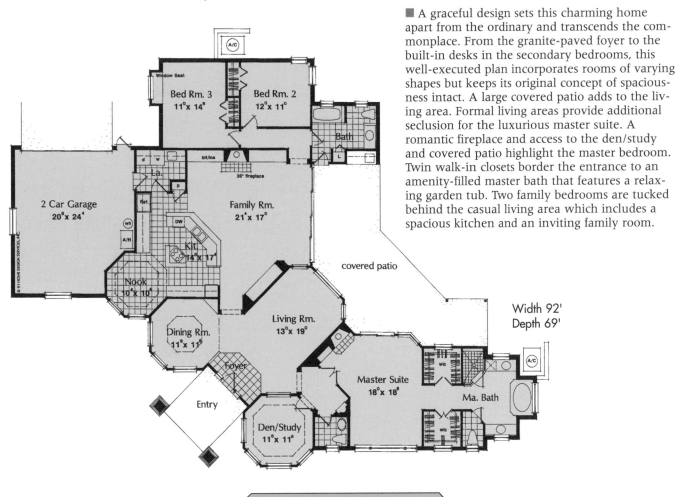

Design 8603

Square Footage: 2,656

■ A graceful design sets this charming home apart from the ordinary and transcends the commonplace. From the granite-paved foyer to the built-in desks in the secondary bedrooms, this well-executed plan incorporates rooms of varying shapes but keeps its original concept of spaciousness intact. A large covered patio adds to the living area. Formal living areas provide additional seclusion for the luxurious master suite. A romantic fireplace and access to the den/study and covered patio highlight the master bedroom. Twin walk-in closets border the entrance to an amenity-filled master bath that features a relaxing garden tub. Two family bedrooms are tucked behind the casual living area which includes a spacious kitchen and an inviting family room.

Width 92'
Depth 69'

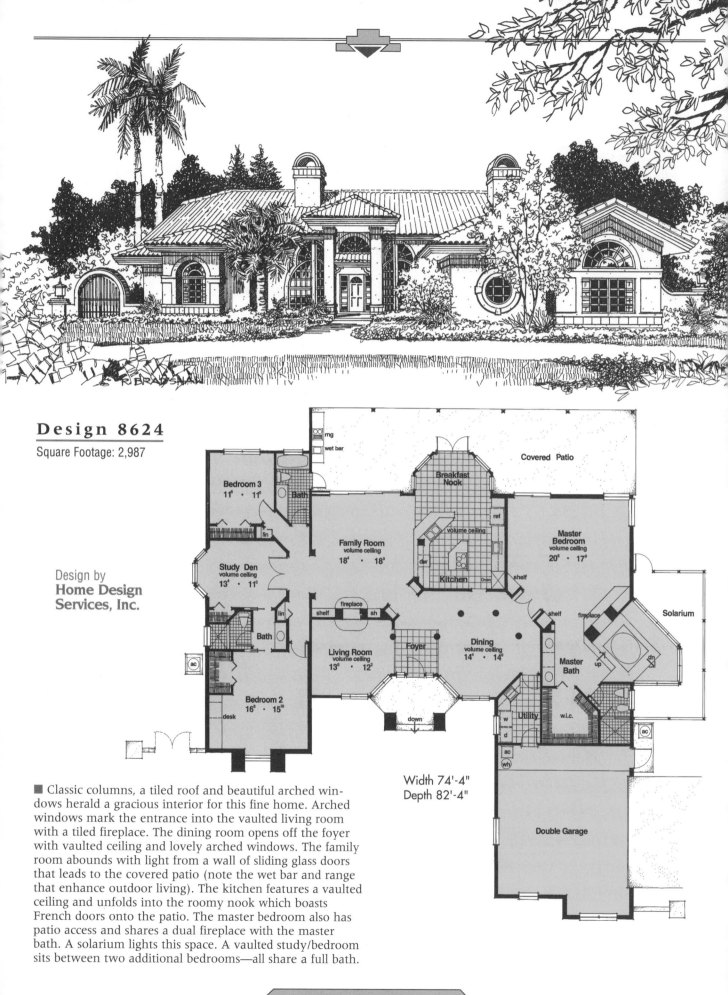

Design 8624

Square Footage: 2,987

Design by
**Home Design
Services, Inc.**

Bedroom 3
$11^6 \cdot 11^0$

Bath

rng

wet bar

Breakfast
Nook

Covered Patio

Family Room
volume ceiling
$18^4 \cdot 18^0$

volume ceiling

ref

Master
Bedroom
volume ceiling
$20^8 \cdot 17^0$

Study Den
volume ceiling
$13^4 \cdot 11^0$

lin

Kitchen

dw

Oven

shelf

lin

shelf

Bath

fireplace

shelf

sh

Living Room
volume ceiling
$13^6 \cdot 12^2$

Foyer

Dining
volume ceiling
$14^4 \cdot 14^0$

shelf

fireplace

Solarium

up

dn

Master
Bath

ac

Bedroom 2
$16^8 \cdot 15^{10}$

desk

down

w

d

Utility

w.l.c.

ac

ac

wh

Width 74'-4"
Depth 82'-4"

Double Garage

■ Classic columns, a tiled roof and beautiful arched windows herald a gracious interior for this fine home. Arched
windows mark the entrance into the vaulted living room
with a tiled fireplace. The dining room opens off the foyer
with vaulted ceiling and lovely arched windows. The family
room abounds with light from a wall of sliding glass doors
that leads to the covered patio (note the wet bar and range
that enhance outdoor living). The kitchen features a vaulted
ceiling and unfolds into the roomy nook which boasts
French doors onto the patio. The master bedroom also has
patio access and shares a dual fireplace with the master
bath. A solarium lights this space. A vaulted study/bedroom
sits between two additional bedrooms—all share a full bath.

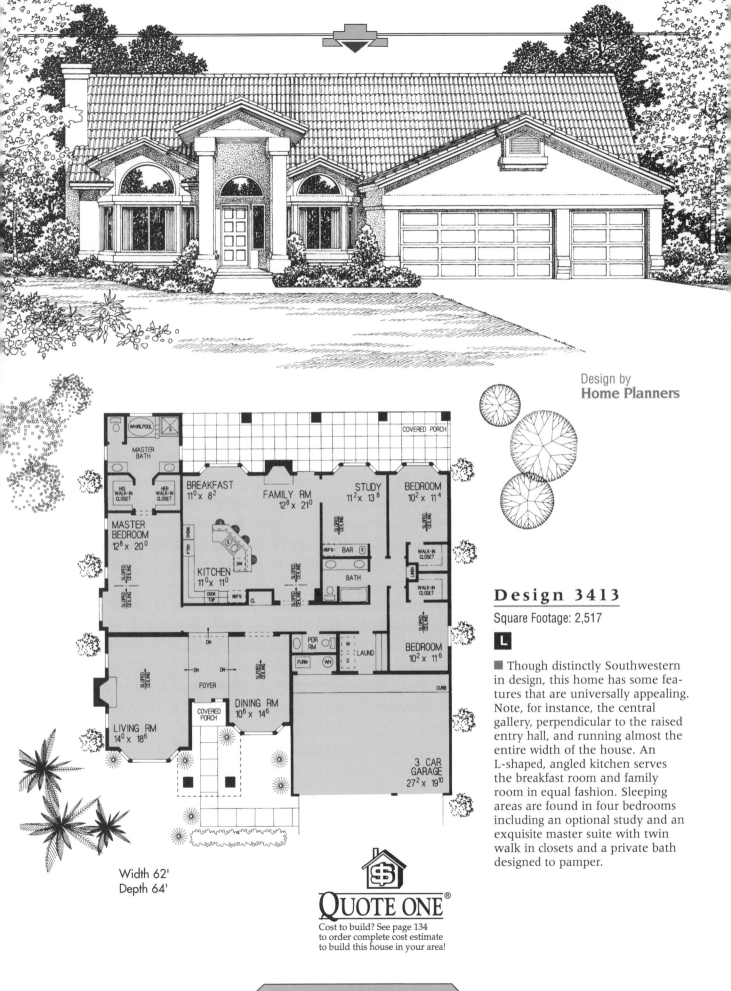

Design by
Home Planners

Design 3413

Square Footage: 2,517

L

■ Though distinctly Southwestern in design, this home has some features that are universally appealing. Note, for instance, the central gallery, perpendicular to the raised entry hall, and running almost the entire width of the house. An L-shaped, angled kitchen serves the breakfast room and family room in equal fashion. Sleeping areas are found in four bedrooms including an optional study and an exquisite master suite with twin walk in closets and a private bath designed to pamper.

Width 62'
Depth 64'

QUOTE ONE®
Cost to build? See page 134
to order complete cost estimate
to build this house in your area!

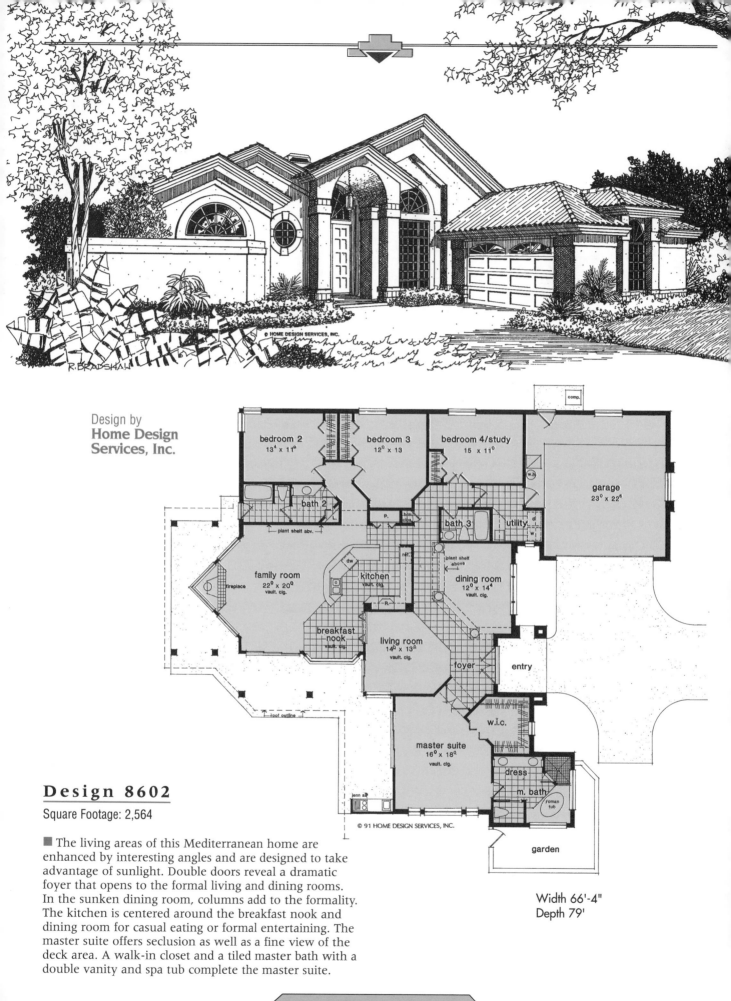

Design by
**Home Design
Services, Inc.**

bedroom 2
13⁴ x 11⁰

bedroom 3
12⁰ x 13

bedroom 4/study
15 x 11⁰

comp.

garage
23⁰ x 22⁶

bath 2

plant shelf abv.

bath 3

utility

plant shelf above

family room
22⁰ x 20⁰
vault. clg.

fireplace

dw

kitchen
vault. clg.

réf.

dining room
12⁰ x 14⁴
vault. clg.

breakfast
nook
vault. clg.

living room
14⁰ x 13⁰
vault. clg.

foyer

entry

roof outline

jenn air

w.i.c.

master suite
16⁰ x 18⁰
vault. clg.

dress

m. bath

roman
tub

garden

© 91 HOME DESIGN SERVICES, INC.

Design 8602

Square Footage: 2,564

■ The living areas of this Mediterranean home are
enhanced by interesting angles and are designed to take
advantage of sunlight. Double doors reveal a dramatic
foyer that opens to the formal living and dining rooms.
In the sunken dining room, columns add to the formality.
The kitchen is centered around the breakfast nook and
dining room for casual eating or formal entertaining. The
master suite offers seclusion as well as a fine view of the
deck area. A walk-in closet and a tiled master bath with a
double vanity and spa tub complete the master suite.

Width 66'-4"
Depth 79'

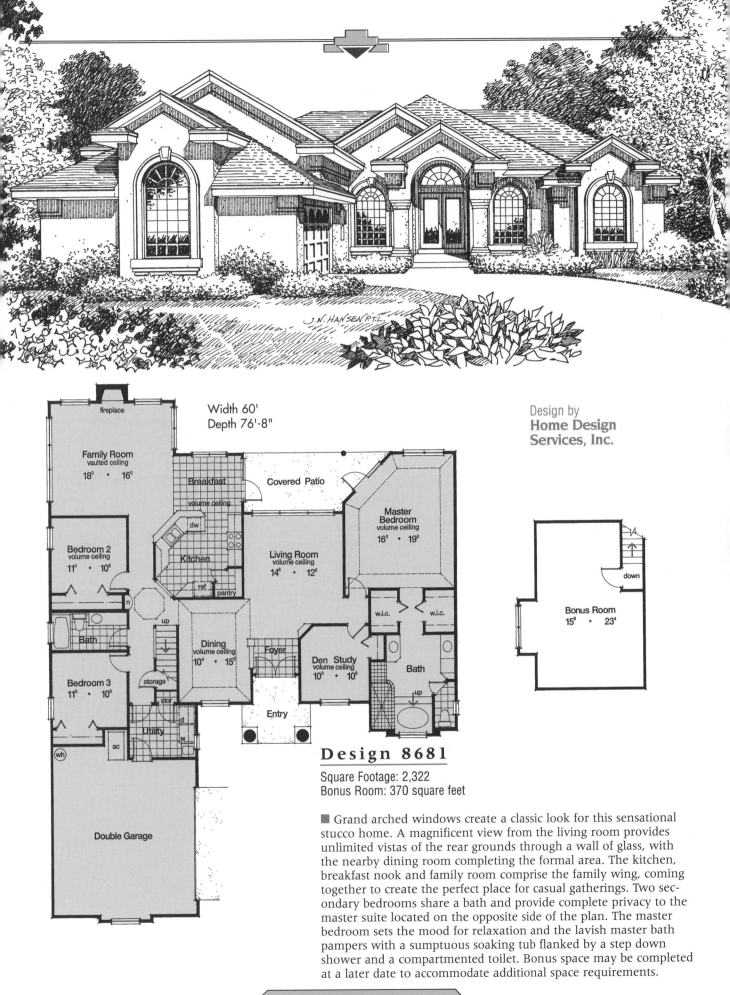

Width 60'
Depth 76'-8"

Design by
**Home Design
Services, Inc.**

fireplace

Family Room
vaulted ceiling
18⁰ • 16⁰

Breakfast
volume ceiling

Covered Patio

**Master
Bedroom**
volume ceiling
16⁰ • 19⁰

dw

Kitchen

Bedroom 2
volume ceiling
11⁰ • 10⁸

Living Room
volume ceiling
14⁸ • 12⁰

ref

pantry

w.i.c.   w.i.c.

up

Bath

Dining
volume ceiling
10⁴ • 15⁰

Foyer

Den Study
volume ceiling
10⁰ • 10⁸

Bath

Bedroom 3
11⁰ • 10⁸

storage

stor

up

Entry

Utility

d

w

ac

wh

Double Garage

down

Bonus Room
15⁸ • 23⁴

Design 8681

Square Footage: 2,322
Bonus Room: 370 square feet

■ Grand arched windows create a classic look for this sensational stucco home. A magnificent view from the living room provides unlimited vistas of the rear grounds through a wall of glass, with the nearby dining room completing the formal area. The kitchen, breakfast nook and family room comprise the family wing, coming together to create the perfect place for casual gatherings. Two secondary bedrooms share a bath and provide complete privacy to the master suite located on the opposite side of the plan. The master bedroom sets the mood for relaxation and the lavish master bath pampers with a sumptuous soaking tub flanked by a step down shower and a compartmented toilet. Bonus space may be completed at a later date to accommodate additional space requirements.

Design 8677

Square Footage: 2,874

■ The columned entry foyer of this classic design leads to an inviting formal living/dining area with a view to the rear yard. Double doors lead to the master suite foyer, which separates the bedroom and bathroom areas. The bath features His and Hers vanities, a doorless shower and unique window design that overlooks a private garden. Secondary bedrooms enjoy back-yard living as does the huge family room and nook. Window seats grace two of the family bedrooms. Conveniently located, a powder room and a pool bath provide additional bath facilities. A three-car garage allows plenty of space for all vehicles.

Design by
Home Design
Services, Inc.

Width 71'-4"
Depth 80'-8"

Design 8618

First Floor: 1,352 square feet
Second Floor: 1,000 square feet
Total: 2,352 square feet

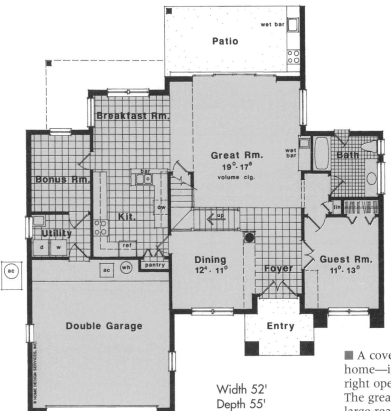

Width 52'
Depth 55'

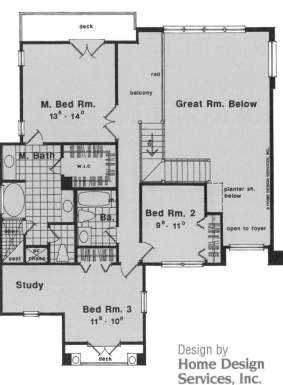

Design by
**Home Design
Services, Inc.**

■ A covered patio shades the entry to the foyer of this home—it is lit by an arched window. Double doors to the right open to a guest room with an arched picture window. The great room—open to the level above—has a wet bar; a large rear patio also offers a wet bar. The tiled kitchen provides a serving bar for the breakfast room. French doors in the master bedroom open onto a deck. The spacious bath here includes a walk-in closet, twin vanities and spa tub. Two additional bedrooms and a bath complete the second level. The front bedroom includes a study and opens onto a deck. The plan can be built with a flat-tiled or barrel roof.

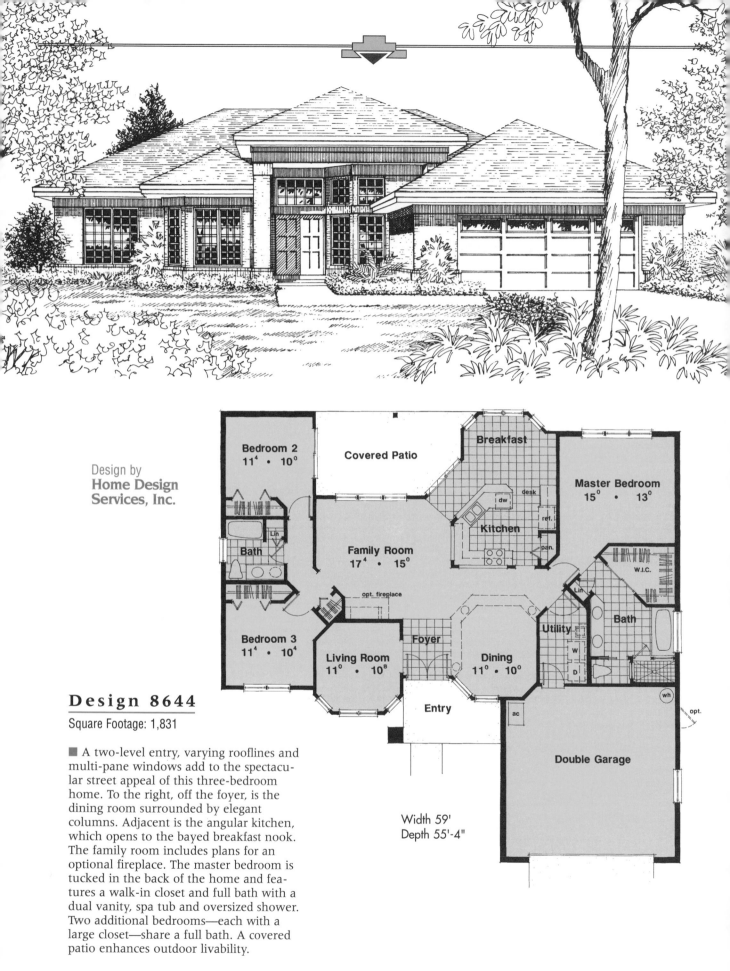

Design by
Home Design Services, Inc.

Design 8644

Square Footage: 1,831

■ A two-level entry, varying rooflines and multi-pane windows add to the spectacular street appeal of this three-bedroom home. To the right, off the foyer, is the dining room surrounded by elegant columns. Adjacent is the angular kitchen, which opens to the bayed breakfast nook. The family room includes plans for an optional fireplace. The master bedroom is tucked in the back of the home and features a walk-in closet and full bath with a dual vanity, spa tub and oversized shower. Two additional bedrooms—each with a large closet—share a full bath. A covered patio enhances outdoor livability.

Width 59'
Depth 55'-4"

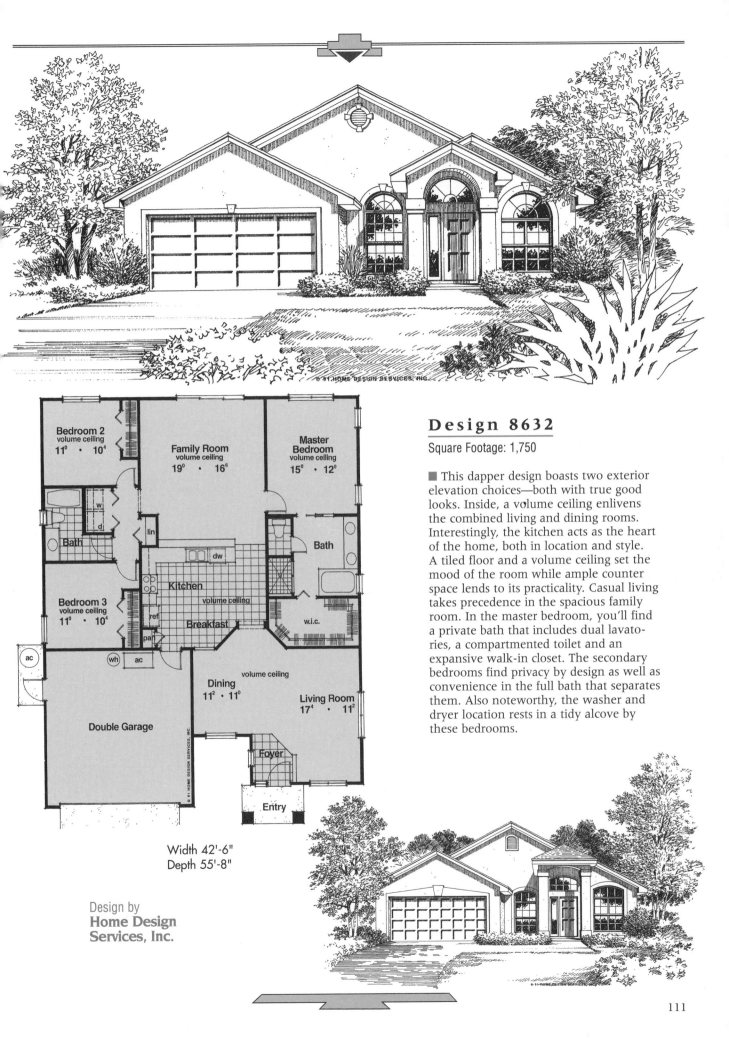

Design 8632

Square Footage: 1,750

■ This dapper design boasts two exterior elevation choices—both with true good looks. Inside, a volume ceiling enlivens the combined living and dining rooms. Interestingly, the kitchen acts as the heart of the home, both in location and style. A tiled floor and a volume ceiling set the mood of the room while ample counter space lends to its practicality. Casual living takes precedence in the spacious family room. In the master bedroom, you'll find a private bath that includes dual lavatories, a compartmented toilet and an expansive walk-in closet. The secondary bedrooms find privacy by design as well as convenience in the full bath that separates them. Also noteworthy, the washer and dryer location rests in a tidy alcove by these bedrooms.

Bedroom 2
volume ceiling
11⁰ · 10⁴

Family Room
volume ceiling
19⁰ · 16⁶

Master Bedroom
volume ceiling
15⁰ · 12⁰

Bath

Kitchen
volume ceiling

Bath

Bedroom 3
volume ceiling
11⁰ · 10⁴

Breakfast

w.i.c.

Double Garage

Dining
11² · 11⁰

volume ceiling

Living Room
17⁴ · 11²

Foyer

Entry

Width 42'-6"
Depth 55'-8"

Design by
**Home Design
Services, Inc.**

Design 3323

First Floor: 1,923 square feet
Second Floor: 838 square feet
Total: 2,761 square feet

L

■ This two-story Southwestern home was designed to make living patterns as pleasant as they can be. Take a step down from the foyer and go where your mood takes you: a gathering room with fireplace and an alcove for reading or quiet conversations, a media room for enjoying the latest technology, or to the dining room with sliding glass doors to the terrace. The kitchen has an island range and eating space. Also on the first floor is a large master suite including a sitting area with terrace access, walk-in closet and whirlpool tub. An elegant spiral staircase leads to two family bedrooms sharing a full bath and a guest bedroom with private bath.

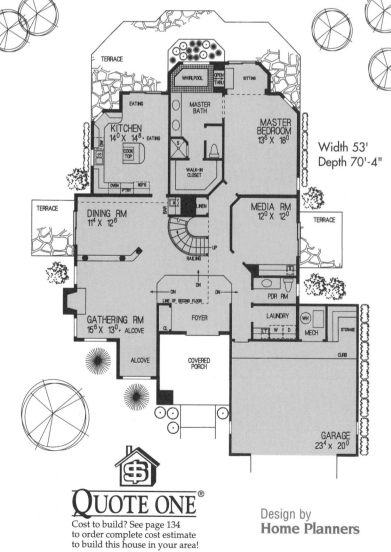

Width 53'
Depth 70'-4"

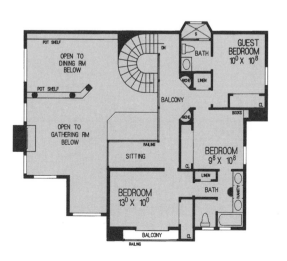

QUOTE ONE®

Cost to build? See page 134 to order complete cost estimate to build this house in your area!

Design by
Home Planners

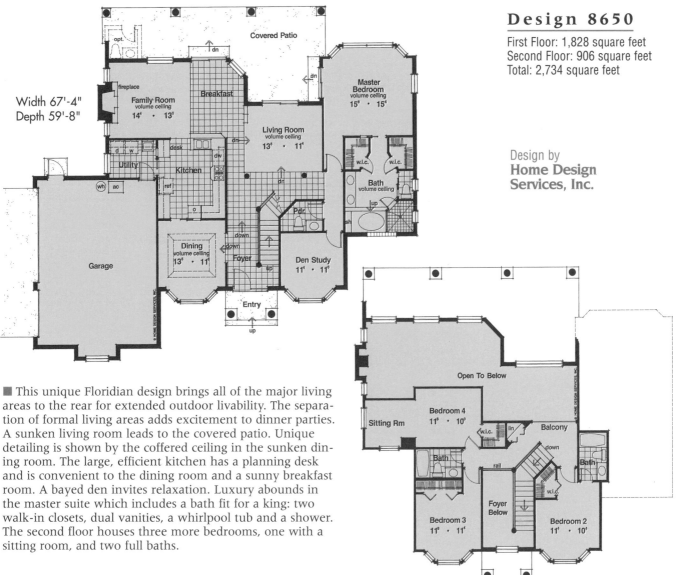

© HOME DESIGN SERVICES, INC.

Width 67'-4"
Depth 59'-8"

Covered Patio

opt.

fireplace

Breakfast

Family Room
volume ceiling
14⁰ · 13⁰

Master Bedroom
volume ceiling
15⁸ · 15⁴

Living Room
volume ceiling
13⁸ · 11⁴

desk

w.i.c.   w.i.c.

Utility

d w

Kitchen

dw

ref

Bath
volume ceiling

wh ac

o

up

Garage

Dining
volume ceiling
13⁰ · 11⁴

Foyer

down
down

up

Pdr.

Den Study
11⁴ · 11⁰

Entry

up

Design 8650

First Floor: 1,828 square feet
Second Floor: 906 square feet
Total: 2,734 square feet

Design by
**Home Design
Services, Inc.**

Open To Below

Sitting Rm

Bedroom 4
11⁸ · 10⁰

w.i.c.   lin

Balcony

Bath

rail

down

Bath

w.i.c.

Bedroom 3
11⁸ · 11⁴

**Foyer
Below**

Bedroom 2
11⁴ · 10⁰

■ This unique Floridian design brings all of the major living areas to the rear for extended outdoor livability. The separation of formal living areas adds excitement to dinner parties. A sunken living room leads to the covered patio. Unique detailing is shown by the coffered ceiling in the sunken dining room. The large, efficient kitchen has a planning desk and is convenient to the dining room and a sunny breakfast room. A bayed den invites relaxation. Luxury abounds in the master suite which includes a bath fit for a king: two walk-in closets, dual vanities, a whirlpool tub and a shower. The second floor houses three more bedrooms, one with a sitting room, and two full baths.

Design 8668

Square Footage: 2,271

■ The handsome lines of this
home create lots of curb appeal.
The double door entry opens to
formal living with a living room
on the left and an elegant dining
room on the right. A spacious
family room with a fireplace opens
to a covered patio. The kitchen
and breakfast room function well
together to make meals a cinch to
prepare and enjoy. The master
suite is located to the rear of the
plan and delights with a bayed sitting area and a luxurious bath.
Three secondary bedrooms share
two full baths. A front facing
garage accesses the home through
a laundry room.

Design by
**Home Design
Services, Inc.**

Width 63'
Depth 53'-4"

SUN-COUNTRY COURTYARDS

Design by
**Larry W. Garnett
& Associates, Inc.**

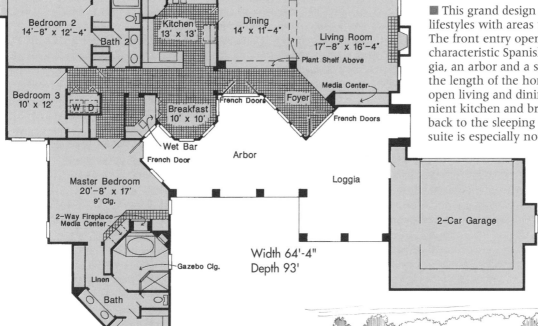

Bedroom 2
14'-8" x 12'-4"

Bath 2

Kitchen
13' x 13'

Dining
14' x 11'-4"

Living Room
17'-8" x 16'-4"

Plant Shelf Above

Media Center

Bedroom 3
10' x 12'

W D

Breakfast
10' x 10'

French Doors

Foyer

French Doors

Wet Bar

French Door

Arbor

Loggia

Master Bedroom
20'-8" x 17'
9' Clg.

2-Way Fireplace
Media Center

2-Car Garage

Gazebo Clg.

Linen

Bath

Width 64'-4"
Depth 93'

Design 9083

Square Footage: 2,176

■ This grand design caters to outdoor lifestyles with areas that invite visitation. The front entry opens to a beautiful and characteristic Spanish courtyard with a loggia, an arbor and a spa area. The foyer runs the length of the home and leads from open living and dining areas to a convenient kitchen and breakfast nook, then back to the sleeping quarters. The master suite is especially notable with its luxurious bath and ample closet space. Note the many extras in the plan: a fireplace and a media center in the living room and in the master bedroom, a wet bar at the breakfast nook, and an oversized pantry in the kitchen.

Design 9082

Square Footage: 2,360

■ Reminiscent of the homes built long ago in the Southwest, this Spanish adaptation contains many components to draw attention to it. A long entry porch leads to an angled foyer flanked by a huge living room with a cathedral ceiling and a dining room with a sloped ceiling. Across the gallery is a long skylit porch that overlooks the tiled courtyard. The kitchen features plenty of counter space and a large pantry. To the rear, in privacy, is the master bedroom suite. It features a tub area with a raised gazebo ceiling and transom windows. There are also two family bedrooms sharing a full bath with double vanities.

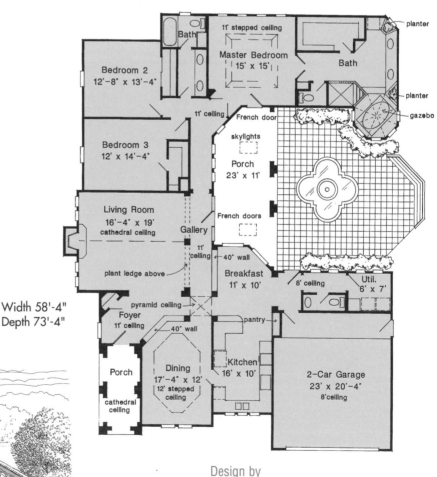

Width 58'-4"
Depth 73'-4"

Bath

11' stepped ceiling

Master Bedroom
15' x 15'

Bath

planter

planter

gazebo ce

Bedroom 2
12'-8" x 13'-4"

11' ceiling

French door

skylights

Porch
23' x 11'

Bedroom 3
12' x 14'-4"

Living Room
16'-4" x 19'
cathedral ceiling

Gallery

French doors

11' ceiling

40" wall

plant ledge above

Breakfast
11' x 10'

8' ceiling

Util.
6' x 7'

pyramid ceiling

Foyer
11' ceiling

40" wall

pantry

Kitchen
16' x 10'

2-Car Garage
23' x 20'-4"
8'ceiling

Porch

cathedral ceiling

Dining
17'-4" x 12'
12' stepped ceiling

Design by
Larry W. Garnett
& Associates, Inc.

Design 3629

Square Footage: 2,966

L

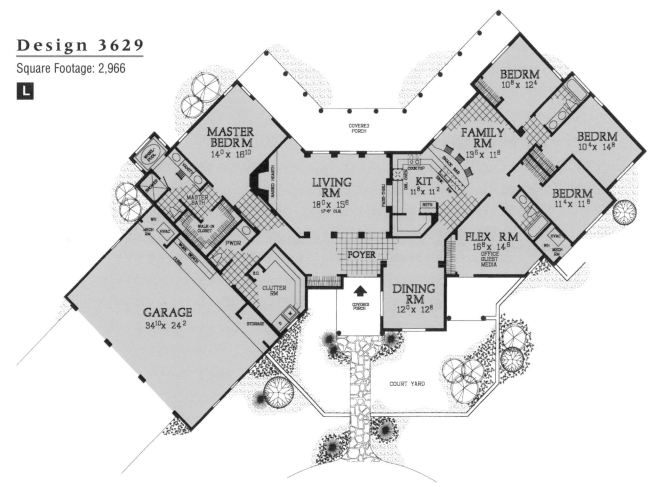

Width 114'-10"
Depth 79'-2"

Design by
Home Planners

■ From its arched entryway to its rear covered porch, this design has a lot to offer. Inside, to the right of the foyer is the formal dining room. Directly ahead, a large and inviting living room has a fireplace and a wall of windows, along with access to the rear porch. The G-shaped kitchen has a huge walk-in pantry, a pass-through to the living room and shares a snack bar with the adjoining family room. Three secondary bedrooms are clustered together off the family room and share two full baths. A flex room with access to the front courtyard is available for an office or guest quarters. Located on the other end of the house, the master bedroom has private access to the rear porch and a lavish bath.

Design 3660

Square Footage: 2,086

L

Design by
Home Planners

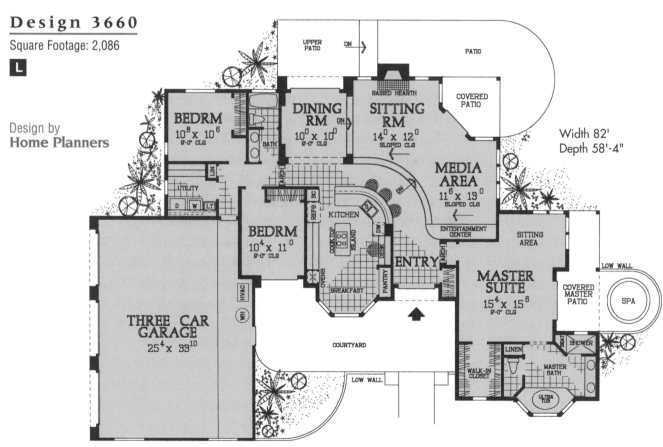

UPPER PATIO

DN

PATIO

RAISED HEARTH

COVERED PATIO

BEDRM
10⁸ x 10⁶
9'-0" CLG

BATH

DINING RM
10⁰ x 10⁰
9'-0" CLG

DN

SITTING RM
14⁰ x 12⁰
SLOPED CLG

Width 82'
Depth 58'-4"

LIN

UTILITY

D W LT

ARCH

REFG BC

KITCHEN

DN

ARCH

MEDIA AREA
11⁶ x 13⁰
SLOPED CLG

ENTERTAINMENT CENTER

SITTING AREA

BEDRM
10⁴ x 11⁰
9'-0" CLG

COOKTOP

ISLAND

DW

DESK

ARCH

LOW WALL

THREE CAR GARAGE
25⁴ x 33¹⁰

HVAC

WH

OVENS

BREAKFAST

PANTRY

ENTRY

MASTER SUITE
15⁴ x 15⁶
9'-0" CLG

COVERED MASTER PATIO

SPA

COURTYARD

WALK-IN CLOSET

LINEN

MASTER BATH

SHOWER

ULTRA TUB

LOW WALL

■ This home exhibits wonderful dual-use space in the sunken sitting room and media area. Anchoring each end of this spacious living zone is the raised-hearth fireplace and the entertainment center. The outstanding kitchen has an informal breakfast bay and looks over the snack bar to the family area. To the rear of the plan, a few steps from the kitchen and functioning with the upper patio, is the formal dining room. Through the archway are two children's bedrooms and a bath with twin vanities. At the far end of the plan is the master suite. It has a sitting area with fine, natural light. A few steps away, French doors open to the covered master patio.

Design by
Home Planners

Design 2804

Square Footage: 1,674

L **D**

■ Stuccoed arches, multi-pane windows and a gracefully sloped roof accent the exterior of this Spanish-inspired design. The foyer leads to each of the living areas. The sleeping area of two—or optional three—bedrooms is ready to serve the family. The interior kitchen will efficiently serve the dining room, covered dining porch and breakfast room with great ease. The gathering room, an impressive 16 x 20 feet, features a fireplace. Special details include a bay window in the front bedroom, snack bar and desk in the breakfast room, and extra storage space in the garage. Blueprints for this design include details for an optional non-basement plan.

Width 68'
Depth 48'-8"

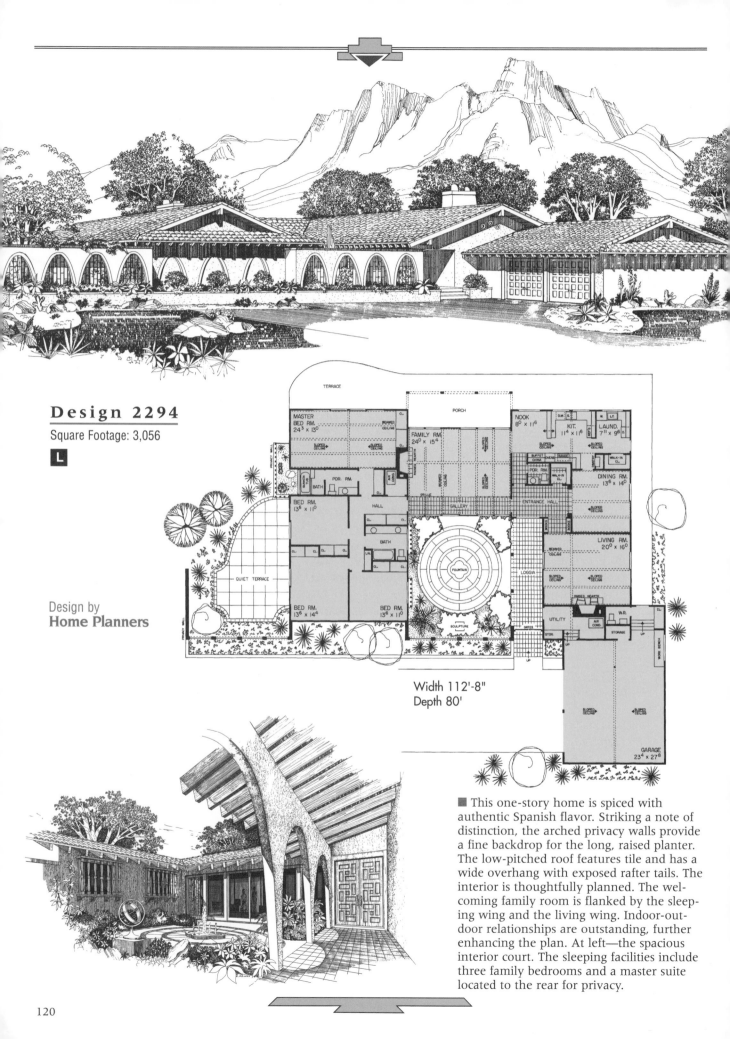

Design 2294

Square Footage: 3,056

L

Design by
Home Planners

Width 112'-8"
Depth 80'

■ This one-story home is spiced with
authentic Spanish flavor. Striking a note of
distinction, the arched privacy walls provide
a fine backdrop for the long, raised planter.
The low-pitched roof features tile and has a
wide overhang with exposed rafter tails. The
interior is thoughtfully planned. The welcoming family room is flanked by the sleeping wing and the living wing. Indoor-outdoor relationships are outstanding, further
enhancing the plan. At left—the spacious
interior court. The sleeping facilities include
three family bedrooms and a master suite
located to the rear for privacy.

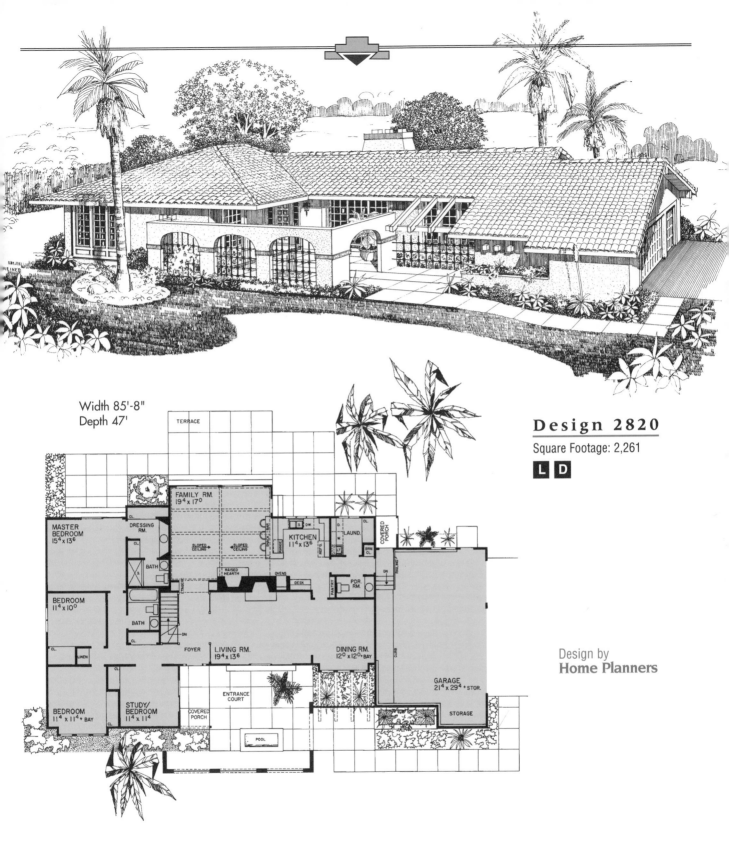

Width 85'-8"
Depth 47'

TERRACE

FAMILY RM.
19⁴ x 17⁰

MASTER
BEDROOM
15⁴ x 13⁶

DRESSING
RM.

CL

CL

SLOPED CEILING

SLOPED CEILING

KITCHEN
11⁴ x 13⁶

COVERED
PORCH

S DW

REF.

D.

LT.

LAUND.

W

BRM.
CL.

BATH

RAISED
HEARTH

OVENS

DESK

DN

RAILING

Design 2820

Square Footage: 2,261

L D

BEDROOM
11⁴ x 10⁰

ETAGERE

PDR.
RM.

PANTRY

BATH

CL

DN

CURB

GARAGE
21⁴ x 29⁴ + STOR.

Design by
Home Planners

LINEN

CL

FOYER

LIVING RM.
19⁴ x 13⁶

DINING RM.
12⁰ x 12⁰ + BAY

BEDROOM
11⁴ x 11⁴ BAY

STUDY/
BEDROOM
11⁴ x 11⁴

CL

ENTRANCE
COURT

COVERED
PORCH

STORAGE

POOL

■ A privacy wall around the courtyard with pool and trellised planter area is a gracious area by which to enter this one-story design. The Spanish flavor is accented by the grillework and the tiled roof. The front living room has sliding glass doors, which open to the entrance court. The adjacent dining room features a bay window.

Informal activities will be enjoyed in the rear family room with a sloped, beamed ceiling, a raised-hearth fireplace, sliding glass doors to the terrace and a snack bar. The sleeping wing can remain quiet away from the plan's activity centers. Notice the three-car garage with extra storage space.

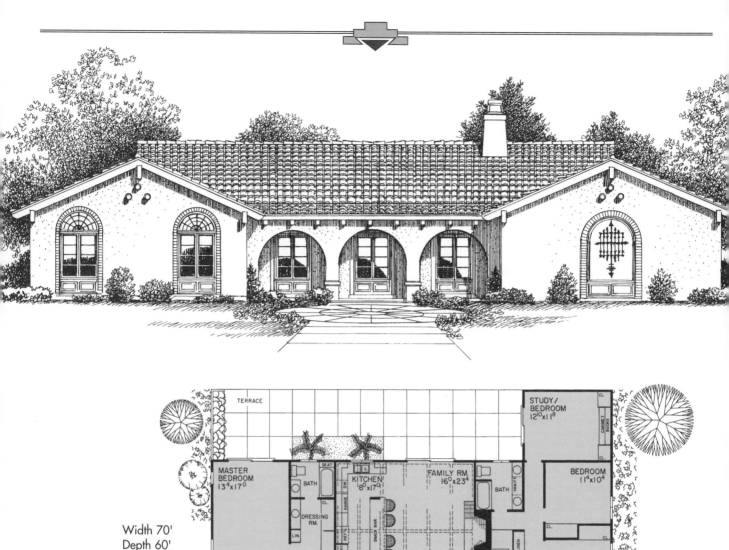

Design 2236

Square Footage: 2,307

■ Traditional Spanish design is used to good measure in this graceful one story home. The entry is graced with arches introducing a covered porch and directs visitors to an offset foyer located to the left. The living room is set down one step from other areas of the home and connects directly to the formal dining room. The family room is at the center of the plan and is open to the L-shaped kitchen that features a snack bar. Family bedrooms are found to the right of the plan. One has built-ins that make it perfect for a study. The master suite features patio access and contains a bath with a dressing room, and dual vanities.

Design by
Home Planners

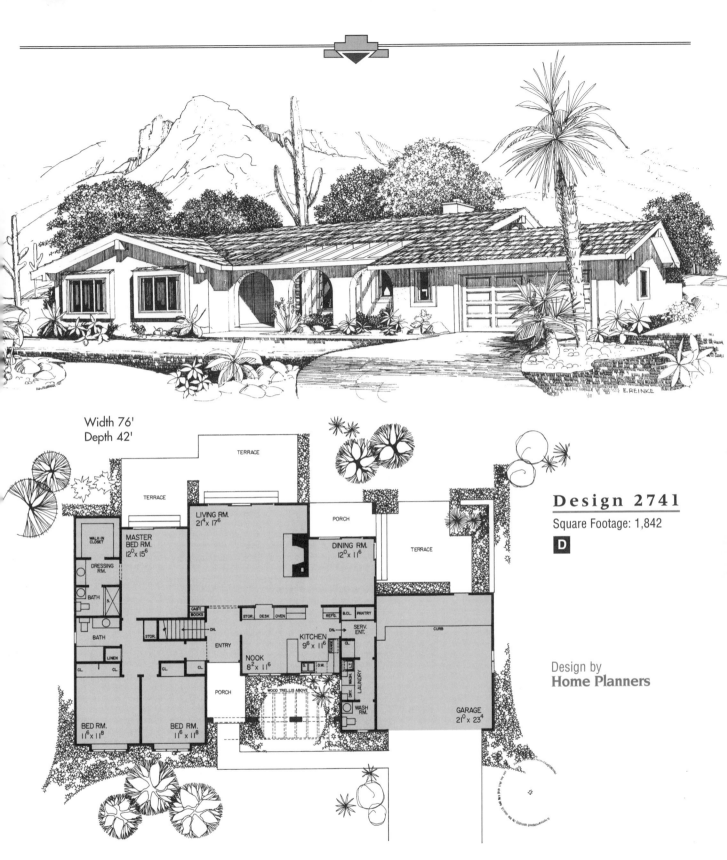

Width 76'
Depth 42'

Design 2741

Square Footage: 1,842

D

Design by
Home Planners

■ From the classic covered courtyard in the front, to the many terraces found at the rear, the outdoor living in this home is perfect for the sunny Southwest. The entry separates living and sleeping zones and allows access to the kitchen/nook area and then beyond to the living room and dining room. Notice there are two outdoor spaces reached from the dining room! The master suite also has outdoor access and offers a walk-in closet, dressing room and dual vanities. Family bedrooms share a full bath. The two-car garage connects to the home via a laundry room and washroom.

Design by
Home Planners

Design 2143

Main Level: 832 square feet
Upper Level: 864 square feet
Lower Level: 864 square feet
Total: 2,560 square feet

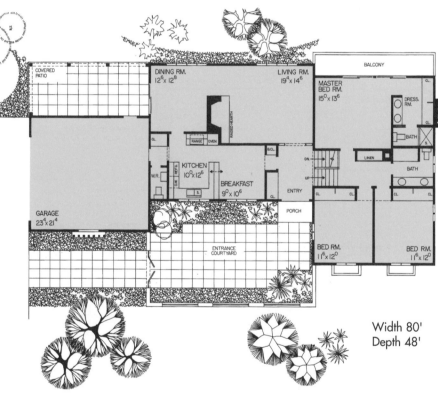

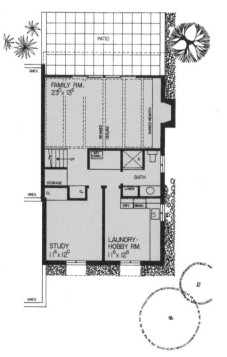

Width 80'
Depth 48'

■ Here, the Spanish Southwest comes to life in the form of an enchanting multi-level home. The architectural detailing is grand. The entrance courtyard, the twin balconies and the roof treatment are particularly noteworthy. At the rear of the house are the covered patio and the balcony with its lower patio. The upper level has three bedrooms and two baths; the main level has formal living and dining rooms to the rear and kitchen area looking onto the courtyard; the lower level features the family room, study and laundry. There are two fireplaces—each with a raised hearth.

Design 2850

Main Level: 1,530 square feet
Upper Level: 984 square feet
Lower Level: 951 square feet
Total: 3,465 square feet

L **D**

■ Partially shielded from the street, the entry court of this Spanish design features planting areas and a small pool. Down six steps from the foyer is the lower level, housing a bedroom and full bath, a study and an activities room. With something for everyone, the activities room enjoys a raised-hearth fireplace, a soda bar and sliding glass doors that open onto a covered terrace. Upper level sleeping quarters are located six steps up from the foyer. The main level accommodates the living areas: formal living and dining rooms, family room, kitchen and adjoining breakfast room, powder room and laundry room. A three-car garage allows plenty of room for the family fleet.

Width 90'
Depth 56'

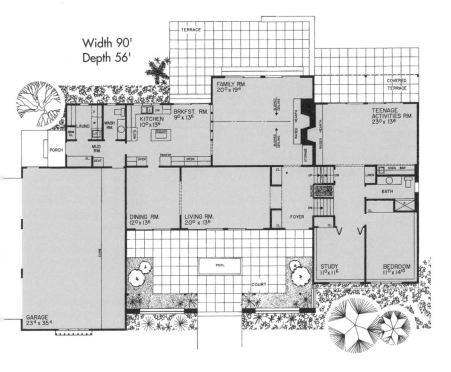

Cost to build? See page 134
to order complete cost estimate
to build this house in your area!

Design by
Home Planners

125

Quote One®

Cost to build? See page 134 to order complete cost estimate to build this house in your area!

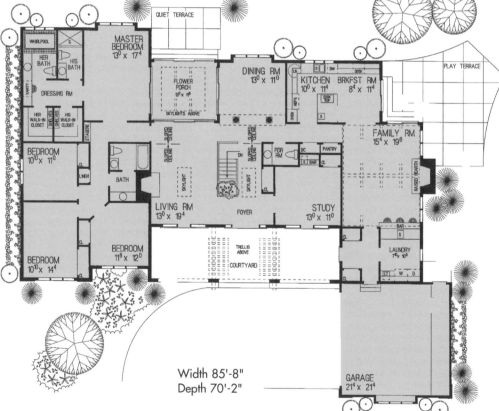

MASTER BEDROOM 13⁰ x 17⁴

QUIET TERRACE

DINING RM 13⁰ x 11⁰

KITCHEN 10⁰ x 11⁴

BRKFST RM 8⁴ x 11⁴

PLAY TERRACE

HER BATH

HIS BATH

DRESSING RM

FLOWER PORCH 13⁰ x 11⁰

SKYLIGHTS ABOVE

WHIRLPOOL

HER WALK-IN CLOSET

HIS WALK-IN CLOSET

FAMILY RM 15⁴ x 19⁸

BEDROOM 10¹⁰ x 11⁰

BATH

SKYLIGHT

LIVING RM 13⁰ x 19⁴

FOYER

STUDY 13⁰ x 11⁰

LINEN

PDR RM

PANTRY

BEDROOM 11⁸ x 12⁰

BEDROOM 10¹⁰ x 14⁴

TRELLIS ABOVE

COURTYARD

LAUNDRY 7⁶ x 10⁸

GARAGE 21⁴ x 21⁴

Design 3344

Square Footage: 3,054

Width 85'-8"
Depth 70'-2"

■ This home features interior planning for today's active family. Living areas include a living room with a fireplace, a cozy study and a family room with a wet bar. Convenient to the kitchen is the formal dining room with an attractive bay window overlooking the back yard. The four-bedroom sleeping area contains a sumptuous master suite. A cheerful flower porch is accessed from the master suite, living room and dining room.

Design by
Home Planners

Design 2922

Square Footage: 3,505

■ Loaded with custom features, this plan seems to have everything imaginable. There's an enormous sunken gathering room and cozy study. The country-style kitchen contains an efficient work area, as well as space for relaxing in the morning and sitting rooms. Two nice-sized bedrooms and a luxurious master suite round out the plan.

Design by
Home Planners

Cost to build? See page 134 to order complete cost estimate to build this house in your area!

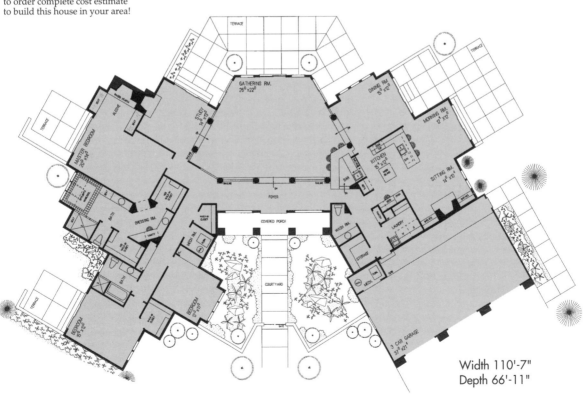

Width 110'-7"
Depth 66'-11"

Design 2200/2677

Square Footage: 1,695/1,634

Design by
Home Planners

Optional
Basement Plan

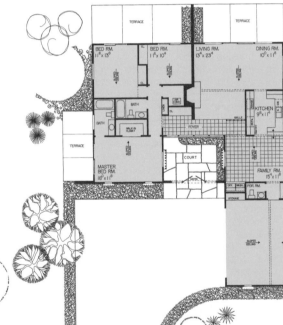

Design 2200

Width 63'-8"
Depth 62'-8"

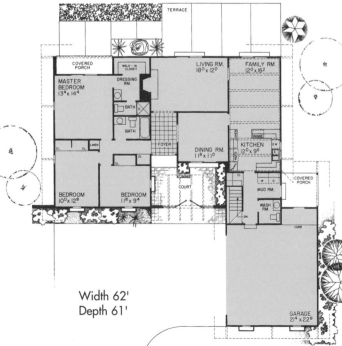

Design 2677

Width 62'
Depth 61'

■ Though different, both floor plans share the stucco exterior of this Spanish-style home enhanced by grill-covered windows and an arched entryway. Interior livability has been well planned in both designs. Design 2200 has a shared living/dining room overlooking the backyard and a front master bedroom with a side terrace, where Design 2677 has a separate front dining room, a family room with access to the rear terrace and a rear master bedroom with an adjacent covered porch. Both designs have two additional bedrooms. Access to the basement varies in each plan. Please specify Design 2200 or Design 2677 when ordering.

Design 2906

First Floor: 2,121 square feet
Second Floor: 913 square feet
Total: 3,034 square feet

L **D**

TERRACE

TERRACE

LAUNDRY
11⁰x9⁴

WASH RM.

KITCHEN
13⁴x13⁴

MUD RM.

PANTRY

OVENS

DESK

FAMILY RM.
18⁰x13⁰

BATH

DRESSING RM.

VANITY

MASTER BEDROOM
11⁰x16⁸

WALK-IN CLOSET

SHLV'S

OPEN THRU FIREPLACE

RAISED HEARTH

DINING RM.
12⁴x13⁴

LOUNGE ABOVE

FOYER

BAR

3 CAR GARAGE
23⁴x37⁰

STORAGE

COVERED PORCH

LIVING RM.
19⁰x19⁰

SLOPED CEILING

COVERED PORCH

STUDY
11⁰x14⁰ + BAY

COURTYARD

Width 84'
Depth 48'

Design by
Home Planners

ROOF

BEDROOM
11⁰x13⁰

BEDROOM
10⁰x10⁰

BATH

CL

LINEN

ATTIC

LOUNGE
19⁴x9⁴

UPPER FOYER

UPPER LIVING RM.

BEDROOM
11⁰x13⁸

RAILING

RAILING

ROOF

ROOF

■ This striking comtemporary design with Spanish good looks offers outstanding livability for today's active lifestyles. A three-car garage opens to a mud room, laundry and wash room. An efficient, spacious kitchen opens to a large dining room, with a pass-through also leading to a family room. The family room and adjoining master bedroom suite overlook a back yard terrace. Just off the master bedroom is a sizable study that opens to a foyer. Stairs just off the foyer make upstairs access quick and easy. The hub of this terrific plan is a living room that faces the front courtyard, and a lounge above the living room. Upstairs, three family bedrooms share a bath and a spacious lounge.

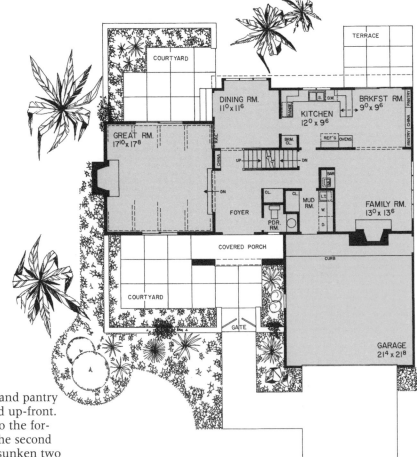

Design by
Home Planners

Design 2801

First Floor: 1,172 square feet
Second Floor: 884 square feet
Total: 2,056 square feet

L **D**

■ Built-ins in the breakfast room for china and pantry goods are certainly features to be mentioned up-front. A second china cabinet is located adjacent to the formal dining room, across from the stairs to the second floor. The great room will be just that. It is sunken two steps, has a beam ceiling, the beauty of a fireplace and two sets of sliding glass doors to a front and rear courtyard. The built-in wet bar and a second fireplace are the features of the family room. The foyer of this Spanish design is very spacious and houses a powder room. Laundry facilities are within the mud room. Four bedrooms and two baths are on the second floor. Don't miss the two enclosed courtyards.

Width 54'-4"
Depth 47'-8"

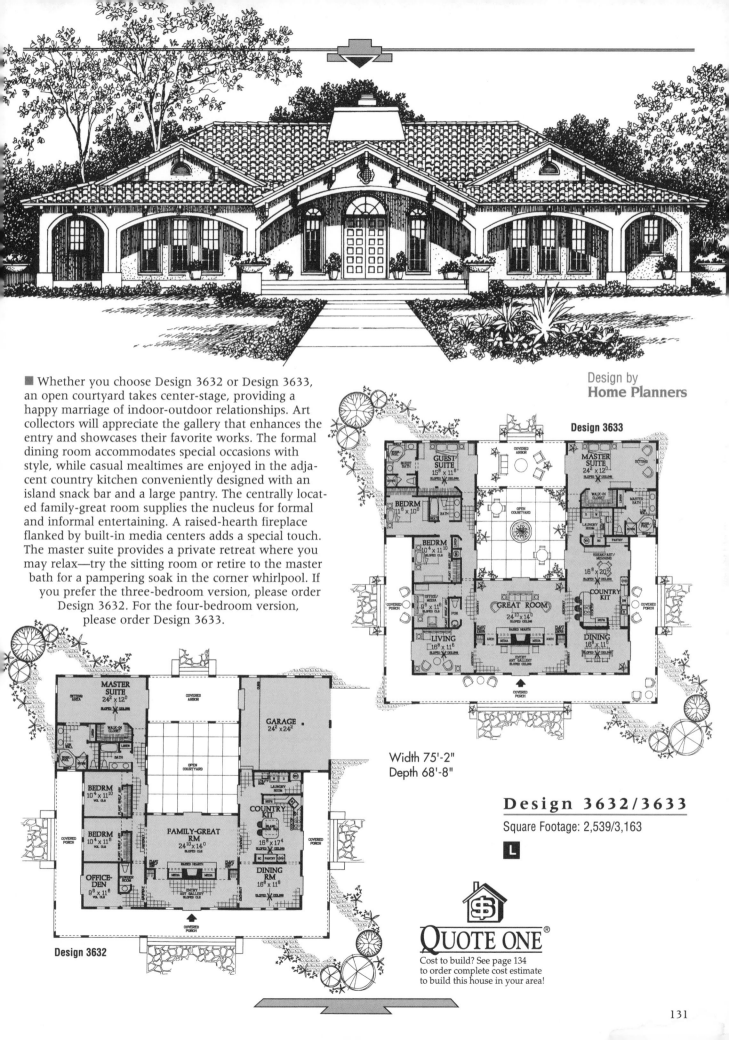

■ Whether you choose Design 3632 or Design 3633, an open courtyard takes center-stage, providing a happy marriage of indoor-outdoor relationships. Art collectors will appreciate the gallery that enhances the entry and showcases their favorite works. The formal dining room accommodates special occasions with style, while casual mealtimes are enjoyed in the adjacent country kitchen conveniently designed with an island snack bar and a large pantry. The centrally located family-great room supplies the nucleus for formal and informal entertaining. A raised-hearth fireplace flanked by built-in media centers adds a special touch. The master suite provides a private retreat where you may relax—try the sitting room or retire to the master bath for a pampering soak in the corner whirlpool. If you prefer the three-bedroom version, please order Design 3632. For the four-bedroom version, please order Design 3633.

Design by
Home Planners

Design 3633

Width 75'-2"
Depth 68'-8"

Design 3632/3633

Square Footage: 2,539/3,163

L

Design 3632

QUOTE ONE®
Cost to build? See page 134 to order complete cost estimate to build this house in your area!

WHEN YOU'RE READY TO ORDER...

LET US SHOW YOU OUR HOME BLUEPRINT PACKAGE.

Building a home? Planning a home? Our Blueprint Package has nearly everything you need to get the job done right, whether you're working on your own or with help from an architect, designer, builder or subcontractors. Each Blueprint Package is the result of many hours of work by licensed architects or professional designers.

QUALITY

Hundreds of hours of painstaking effort have gone into the development of your blueprint set. Each home has been quality-checked by professionals to insure accuracy and buildability.

VALUE

Because we sell in volume, you can buy professional quality blueprints at a fraction of their development cost. With our plans, your dream home design costs only a few hundred dollars, not the thousands of dollars that architects charge.

SERVICE

Once you've chosen your favorite home plan, you'll receive fast, efficient service whether you choose to mail or fax your order to us or call us toll free at 1-800-521-6797. For customer service, call toll free 1-888-690-1116.

SATISFACTION

Over 50 years of service to satisfied home plan buyers provide us unparalleled experience and knowledge in producing quality blueprints.

ORDER TOLL FREE 1-800-521-6797

After you've looked over our Blueprint Package and Important Extras on the following pages, simply mail the order form on page 141 or call toll free on our Blueprint Hotline: 1-800-521-6797. We're ready and eager to serve you. For customer service, call toll free 1-888-690-1116.

Each set of blueprints is an interrelated collection of detail sheets which includes components such as floor plans, interior and exterior elevations, dimensions, cross-sections, diagrams and notations. These sheets show exactly how your house is to be built.

AMONG THE SHEETS INCLUDED MAY BE:

FRONTAL SHEET

This artist's sketch of the exterior of the house gives you an idea of how the house will look when built and landscaped. Large floor plans show all levels of the house and provide an overview of your new home's livability, as well as a handy reference for deciding on furniture placement.

FOUNDATION PLANS

This sheet shows the foundation layout including support walls, excavated and unexcavated areas, if any, and foundation notes. If slab construction rather than basement, the plan shows footings and details for a monolithic slab. This page, or another in the set, may include a sample plot plan for locating your house on a building site.

DETAILED FLOOR PLANS

These plans show the layout of each floor of the house. Rooms and interior spaces are carefully dimensioned and keys are given for cross-section details provided later in the plans. The positions of electrical outlets and switches are shown.

HOUSE CROSS-SECTIONS

Large-scale views show sections or cut-aways of the foundation, interior walls, exterior walls, floors, stairways and roof details. Additional cross-sections may show important changes in floor, ceiling or roof heights or the relationship of one level to another. Extremely valuable for construction, these sections show exactly how the various parts of the house fit together.

INTERIOR ELEVATIONS

Many of our drawings show the design and placement of kitchen and bathroom cabinets, laundry areas, fireplaces, bookcases and other built-ins. Little "extras," such as mantelpiece and wainscoting drawings, plus molding sections, provide details that give your home that custom touch.

EXTERIOR ELEVATIONS

These drawings show the front, rear and sides of your house and give necessary notes on exterior materials and finishes. Particular attention is given to cornice detail, brick and stone accents or other finish items that make your home unique.

SAMPLE PACKAGE

FRONTAL SHEET

FOUNDATION PLANS

DETAILED FLOOR PLANS

EXTERIOR ELEVATIONS

INTERIOR ELEVATIONS

HOUSE CROSS-SECTIONS

INTRODUCING
EIGHT IMPORTANT
PLANNING AND
CONSTRUCTION AIDS
DEVELOPED BY OUR
PROFESSIONALS TO
HELP YOU SUCCEED
IN YOUR HOME-
BUILDING PROJECT

MATERIALS LIST

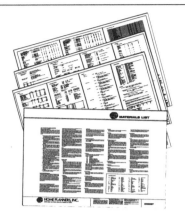

(Note: Because of the diversity of local building codes, our Materials List does not include mechanical materials.)

For many of the designs in our portfolio, we offer a customized materials take-off that is invaluable in planning and estimating the cost of your new home. This Materials List outlines the quantity, type and size of materials needed to build your house (with the exception of mechanical system items). Included are framing lumber, windows and doors, kitchen and bath cabinetry, rough and finish hardware, and much more. This handy list helps you or your builder cost out materials and serves as a reference sheet when you're compiling bids. A Materials List cannot be ordered before blueprints are ordered.

SPECIFICATION OUTLINE

This valuable 16-page document is critical to building your house correctly. Designed to be filled in by you or your builder, this book lists 166 stages or items crucial to the building process. It provides a comprehensive review of the construction process and helps in choosing materials. When combined with the blueprints, a signed contract, and a schedule, it becomes a legal document and record for the building of your home.

QUOTE ONE®

SUMMARY COST REPORT / MATERIALS COST REPORT

A new service for estimating the cost of building select designs, the Quote One® system is available in two separate stages: The Summary Cost Report and the Materials Cost Report.

The **Summary Cost Report** is the first stage in the package and shows the total cost per square foot for your chosen home in your zip-code area and then breaks that cost down into various categories showing the costs for building materials, labor and installation. The report includes three grades: Budget, Standard and Custom. These reports allow you to evaluate your building budget and compare the costs of building a variety of homes in your area.

Make even more informed decisions about your home-building project with the second phase of our package, our **Materials Cost Report.** This tool is invaluable in planning and estimating the cost of your new home. The material and installation (labor and equipment) cost is shown for each of over 1,000 line items provided in the Materials List (Standard grade), which is included when you purchase this estimating tool. It allows you to determine building costs for your specific zip-code area and for your chosen home design. Space is allowed for additional estimates from contractors and subcontractors, such as for mechanical materials, which are not included in our packages. This invaluable tool includes a Materials List. For most plans, a Materials Cost Report cannot be ordered before blueprints are ordered. Call for details. In addition, ask about our Home Planners Estimating Package.

The Quote One® program is continually updated with new plans. If you are interested in a plan that is not indicated as Quote One®, please call and ask our sales reps. They will be happy to verify the status for you. To order these invaluable reports, use the order form on page 141 or call 1-800-521-6797.

CONSTRUCTION INFORMATION

If you want to know more about techniques—and deal more confidently with subcontractors—we offer these useful sheets. Each set is an excellent tool that will add to your understanding of these technical subjects. These helpful details provide general construction information and are not specific to any single plan.

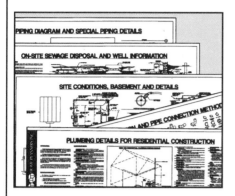

PLUMBING

The Blueprint Package includes locations for all the plumbing fixtures, including sinks, lavatories, tubs, showers, toilets, laundry trays and water heaters. However, if you want to know more about the complete plumbing system, these Plumbing Details will prove very useful. Prepared to meet requirements of the National Plumbing Code, these fact-filled sheets give general information on pipe schedules, fittings, sump-pump details, water-softener hookups, septic system details and much more. Sheets also include a glossary of terms.

ELECTRICAL

The locations for every electrical switch, plug and outlet are shown in your Blueprint Package. However, these Electrical Details go further to take the mystery out of household electrical systems. Prepared to meet requirements of the National Electrical Code, these comprehensive drawings come packed with helpful information, including wire sizing, switch-installation schematics, cable-routing details, appliance wattage, doorbell hookups, typical service panel circuitry and much more. A glossary of terms is also included.

CONSTRUCTION

The Blueprint Package contains everything an experienced builder needs to construct a particular house. However, it doesn't show all the ways that houses can be built, nor does it explain alternate construction methods. To help you understand how your house will be built—and offer additional techniques—this set of Construction Details depicts the materials and methods used to build foundations, fireplaces, walls, floors and roofs. Where appropriate, the drawings show acceptable alternatives.

MECHANICAL

These Mechanical Details contain fundamental principles and useful data that will help you make informed decisions and communicate with subcontractors about heating and cooling systems. Drawings contain instructions and samples that allow you to make simple load calculations, and preliminary sizing and costing analysis. Covered are today's most commonly used systems from heat pumps to solar fuel systems. The package is filled with illustrations and diagrams to help you visualize components and how they relate to one another.

PLAN-A-HOME®

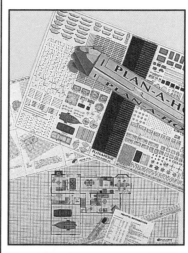

PLAN-A-HOME® is an easy-to-use tool that helps you design a new home, arrange furniture in a new or existing home, or plan a remodeling project. Each package contains:

✓ MORE THAN 700 REUSABLE PEEL-OFF PLANNING SYMBOLS on a self-stick vinyl sheet, including walls, windows, doors, all types of furniture, kitchen components, bath fixtures and many more.

✓ A REUSABLE, TRANSPARENT, ¼" SCALE PLANNING GRID that matches the scale of actual working drawings (¼" equals one foot). This grid provides the basis for house layouts of up to 140'x92'.

✓ TRACING PAPER and a protective sheet for copying or transferring your completed plan.

✓ A FELT-TIP PEN, with water-soluble ink that wipes away quickly.

Plan-A-Home® lets you lay out areas as large as a 7,500 square foot, six-bedroom, seven-bath house.

To Order, Call Toll Free 1-800-521-6797

To add these important extras to your Blueprint Package, simply indicate your choices on the order form on page 141. Or call us toll free 1-800-521-6797 and we'll tell you more about these exciting products. For customer service, call toll free 1-888-690-1116.

THE FINISHING TOUCHES...

THE DECK BLUEPRINT PACKAGE

Many of the homes in this book can be enhanced with a professionally designed Home Planners Deck Plan. Those home plans highlighted with a **D** have a matching Deck Plan, sold separately, which includes a Deck Plan Frontal Sheet, Deck Framing and Floor Plans, Deck Elevations and a Deck Materials List. A Standard Deck Details Package, also available, provides all the how-to information necessary for building *any* deck. Our Complete Deck Building Package contains one set of Custom Deck Plans of your choice, plus one set of Standard Deck Building Details, all for one low price. Our plans and details are carefully prepared in an easy-to-understand format that will guide you through every stage of your deck-building project. This page contains a sampling of six different Deck layouts (and a front-yard landscape) to match your favorite house. See page 138 for prices and ordering information.

EUROPEAN-FLAIR HOME
Landscape OLA088

WEEKEND-ENTERTAINER DECK
Deck ODA013

CENTER-VIEW DECK
Deck ODA015

KITCHEN-EXTENDER DECK
Deck ODA016

SPLIT-LEVEL ACTIVITY DECK
Deck ODA018

TRI-LEVEL DECK WITH GRILL
Deck ODA020

CONTEMPORARY LEISURE DECK
Deck ODA021

For the homes marked with an **L** in this book, Home Planners has created a front-yard Landscape Plan that matches or is complementary in design to the house plan. These comprehensive blueprint packages include a Frontal Sheet, Plan View, Regionalized Plant & Materials List, a sheet on Planting and Maintaining Your Landscape, Zone Maps and Plant Size and Description Guide. These plans will help you achieve professional results, adding value and enjoyment to your property for years to come. Each set of blueprints is a full 18" x 24" in size with clear, complete instructions and easy-to-read type. Six of the forty front-yard Landscape Plans to match your favorite house are shown below.

Regional Order Map

Most of the Landscape Plans shown on these pages are available with a Plant & Materials List adapted by horticultural experts to 8 different regions of the country. Please specify the Geographic Region when ordering your plan. See pages 138–139 for prices, ordering information and regional availability.

Region	1	Northeast
Region	2	Mid-Atlantic
Region	3	Deep South
Region	4	Florida & Gulf Coast
Region	5	Midwest
Region	6	Rocky Mountains
Region	7	Southern California & Desert Southwest
Region	8	Northern California & Pacific Northwest

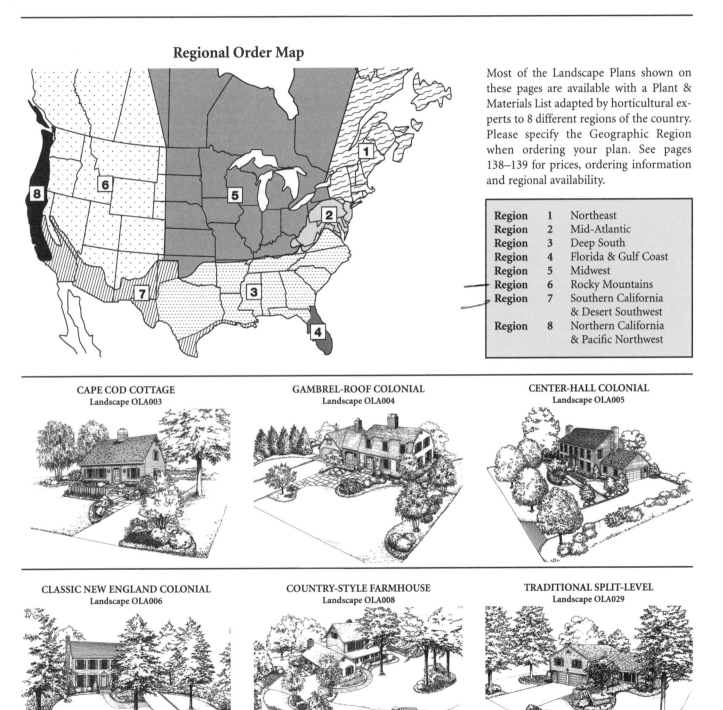

CAPE COD COTTAGE
Landscape OLA003

GAMBREL-ROOF COLONIAL
Landscape OLA004

CENTER-HALL COLONIAL
Landscape OLA005

CLASSIC NEW ENGLAND COLONIAL
Landscape OLA006

COUNTRY-STYLE FARMHOUSE
Landscape OLA008

TRADITIONAL SPLIT-LEVEL
Landscape OLA029

HOUSE BLUEPRINT PRICE SCHEDULE

Prices guaranteed through December 31, 2001

TIERS	1-SET STUDY PACKAGE	4-SET BUILDING PACKAGE	8-SET BUILDING PACKAGE	1-SET REPRODUCIBLE	HOME CUSTOMIZER® PACKAGE
P1	$20	$50	$90	$140	N/A
P2	$40	$70	$110	$160	N/A
P3	$60	$90	$130	$180	N/A
P4	$80	$110	$150	$200	N/A
P5	$100	$130	$170	$230	N/A
P6	$120	$150	$190	$250	N/A
A1	$420	$460	$520	$625	$680
A2	$460	$500	$560	$685	$740
A3	$500	$540	$600	$745	$800
A4	$540	$580	$640	$805	$860
C1	$585	$625	$685	$870	$925
C2	$625	$665	$725	$930	$985
C3	$675	$715	$775	$980	$1035
C4	$725	$765	$825	$1030	$1085
L1	$785	$825	$885	$1090	$1145
L2	$835	$875	$935	$1140	$1195
L3	$935	$975	$1035	$1240	$1295
L4	$1035	$1075	$1135	$1340	$1395

OPTIONS FOR PLANS IN TIERS A1–L4

Additional Identical Blueprints in same order for "A1–L4" price plans ....$50 per set

Reverse Blueprints (mirror image) with 4- or 8-set order
for "A1–L4" price plans ....$50 fee per order

Specification Outlines ....$10 each

Materials Lists for "A1–C3" price plans ....$60 each

Materials Lists for "C4–L4" price plans ....$70 each

OPTIONS FOR PLANS IN TIERS P1–P6

Additional Identical Blueprints in same order for "P1–P6" price plans ....$10 per set

Reverse Blueprints (mirror image) for "P1–P6" price plans ....$10 per set

1 Set of Deck Construction Details ....$14.95 each

Deck Construction Package ....add $10 to Building Package price
(includes 1 set of "P1–P6" price plans, plus
1 set Standard Deck Construction Details)

1 Set of Gazebo Construction Details ....$14.95 each

Gazebo Construction Package ....add $10 to Building Package price
(includes 1 set of "P1–P6" price plans, plus
1 set Standard Gazebo Construction Details)

IMPORTANT NOTES

The 1-set study package is marked "not for construction."
Prices for 4- or 8-set Building Packages honored only at time of original order. Some basement foundations carry a $225 surcharge. Right-reading reverse blueprints, if available, will incur a $165 surcharge.

INDEX

To use the Index below, refer to the design number listed in numerical order (a helpful page reference is also given). Note the price index letter and refer to the House Blueprint Price Schedule above for the cost of one, four or eight sets of blueprints or the cost of a reproducible drawing. Additional prices are shown for identical and reverse blueprint sets, as well as a very useful Materials List for some of the plans. Also note in the Index below those plans that have matching or complementary Deck Plans or Landscape Plans. Refer to the schedules above for prices of these plans. All plans in this publication are customizable. However, only Home Planners

plans can be customized with the Home Planners Home Customizer® Package. These plans are indicated below with the letter "Y." See page 141 for more information. The letter "Y" also identifies plans that are part of our Quote One® estimating service and those that offer Materials Lists. See page 134 for more information.

To Order: Fill in and send the order form on page 141—or call toll free 1-800-521-6797 or 520-297-8200. FAX: 1-800-224-6699 or 520-544-3086

DESIGN	PRICE	PAGE	MATERIALS LIST	CUSTOMIZABLE	QUOTE ONE	DECK	DECK PRICE	LANDSCAPE	LANDSCAPE PRICE	REGIONS
3409	C1	41	Y	Y	Y			OLA031	P4	12345678
3411	C2	77	Y	Y	Y			OLA034	P3	347
3413	C1	105	Y	Y	Y			OLA039	P3	3478
3414	C3	43	Y	Y	Y			OLA034	P3	347
3419	C1	78	Y	Y	Y			OLA040	P4	12345678
3421	A4	73	Y	Y	Y			OLA039	P3	3478
3422	A3	74	Y	Y	Y			OLA040	P4	12345678
3423	C1	60	Y	Y	Y					
3424	C3	45	Y	Y	Y			OLA034	P3	347
3425	C2	39	Y	Y	Y					
3429	C2	44	Y	Y	Y			OLA034	P3	347
3430	A4	79	Y	Y	Y			OLA034	P3	347
3431	A4	6	Y	Y	Y					
3432	C2	25	Y	Y	Y			OLA034	P3	347
3433	C1	9	Y	Y	Y			OLA014	P4	12345678
3434	C2	10	Y	Y	Y			OLA034	P3	347
3435	C3	29	Y	Y	Y			OLA028	P4	12345678
3436	C1	82	Y	Y	Y			OLA028	P4	12345678
3437	A4	26	Y	Y	Y			OLA013	P4	12345678
3440	A4	64	Y	Y	Y			OLA034	P3	347
3441	C1	37	Y	Y	Y			OLA040	P4	12345678
3447	C3	81	Y	Y	Y			OLA038	P3	7
3449	C1	36	Y	Y	Y			OLA037	P4	347
3463	A4	88	Y	Y	Y			OLA039	P3	3478
3464	C3	89	Y	Y	Y	ODA011	P2	OLA034	P3	347
3475	C2	90	Y	Y	Y			OLA037	P4	347
3478	C1	75	Y	Y	Y			OLA039	P3	3478
3480	C1	61	Y	Y	Y	ODA013	P2	OLA039	P3	3478
3486	A3	18	Y	Y	Y					
3562	A4	47	Y	Y	Y	ODA011	P2	OLA039	P3	3478
3563	A3	46	Y	Y	Y	ODA016	P2	OLA034	P3	347
3565	A4	42	Y	Y	Y	ODA011	P2	OLA034	P3	347
3569	A3	76	Y	Y	Y	ODA006	P2	OLA039	P3	3478
3602	C2	91	Y	Y	Y			OLA021	P3	123568
3603	C1	91	Y	Y	Y			OLA021	P3	123568
3628	A4	27	Y	Y						
3629	C1	117	Y	Y				OLA040	P4	12345678
3630	C3	34	Y	Y	Y			OLA010	P3	1234568
3631	C2	92	Y	Y	Y			OLA015	P4	123568
3632	C2	131	Y	Y	Y			OLA038	P3	7
3633	C3	131	Y	Y	Y			OLA038	P3	7
3638	C3	48	Y	Y	Y			OLA016	P4	1234568
3639	C2	35	Y	Y	Y			OLA018	P3	12345678
3640	C2	53	Y	Y	Y			OLA087	P4	12345678
3641	C3	52	Y	Y	Y			OLA031	P4	12345678
3642	C3	8	Y	Y	Y					
3643	C2	16	Y	Y	Y			OLA038	P3	7
3644	C1	15	Y	Y	Y					
3645	C1	28	Y	Y	Y			OLA038	P3	7
3646	C1	11	Y	Y	Y			OLA038	P3	7
3660	C1	118	Y	Y	Y			OLA037	P4	347
3661	A4	49	Y	Y	Y			OLA089	P4	12345678
3665	C1	58	Y	Y	Y			OLA089	P4	12345678
3692	C1	23	Y	Y	Y			OLA091	P3	12345678
3693	C4	7	Y	Y	Y					
3694	C1	30	Y	Y	Y			OLA038	P3	7
3800	C3	20	Y	Y	Y			OLA038	P3	7
3801	C1	17	Y	Y	Y					
6663	C2	84	Y							
8602	C1	106								
8603	C2	103								
8604	A4	102								
8618	A4	109								
8624	C2	104								
8625	C2	85								
8630	A4	67								
8632	A4	111								
8633	A4	66								
8636	C1	97								
8644	A4	110								
8649	C1	100								
8650	C1	113								
8662	C1	94								
8667	A4	96								
8668	A4	114								
8669	C1	99								
8672	C1	93								
8673	A4	98								
8674	A4	38								
8676	C1	101								
8677	C1	108								
8678	C2	55								
8681	C1	107								
8683	C2	95								
9082	A4	116								
9083	A4	115	Y		Y					
9578	A4	56	Y		Y					
9737	A3	65	Y							
9740	A3	59	Y							
9744	A4	69	Y							
HPT464001	C1	68	Y					OLA005	P3	123568
K103	C1	51								
K110	L1	50								
K115	C2	19								
K116	C2	21								
K118	C1	70								
K119	C2	71								

BEFORE YOU ORDER...

OUR EXCHANGE POLICY

Since blueprints are printed in response to your order, we cannot honor requests for refunds. However, we will exchange your entire first order for an equal or greater number of blueprints within our plan collection within 90 days of the original order. The entire content of your original order must be returned to our offices before an exchange will be processed. If the returned blueprints look used, redlined or copied, we will not honor your exchange. Fees for exchanging your blueprints are as follows: 20% of the amount of the original order...*plus* the difference in cost if exchanging for a design in a higher price bracket or *less* the difference in cost if exchanging for a design in lower price bracket. **(Reproducible blueprints are not exchangeable.)** Please add $25 for postage and handling via Regular Service; $35 via Priority Service; $45 via Express Service. Shipping and handling charges are not refundable.

ABOUT REVERSE BLUEPRINTS

If you want to build in reverse of the plan as shown, we will include any number of reverse blueprints (mirror image) from a 4- or 8-set package for an additional fee of $50. Although lettering and dimensions will appear backward, reverses will be a useful aid if you decide to flop the plan.

REVISING, MODIFYING AND CUSTOMIZING PLANS

The wide variety of designs available in this publication allows you to select ideas and concepts for a home to fit your building site and match your family's needs, wants and budget. Like many homeowners who buy these plans, you and your builder, architect or engineer may want to make changes to them. Some changes may be made by your builder, but we recommend that most changes be made by a licensed architect or engineer. If you need to make alterations to a design that is customizable, you need only order our Home Customizer® Package to get you started. As set forth below, we cannot assume any responsibility for blueprints which have been changed, whether by you, your builder or by professionals selected by you or referred to you by us, because such individuals are outside our supervision and control.

ARCHITECTURAL AND ENGINEERING SEALS

Some cities and states are now requiring that a licensed architect or engineer review and "seal" a blueprint, or officially approve it, prior to construction due to concerns over energy costs, safety and other factors. Prior to application for a building permit or the start of actual construction, we strongly advise that you consult your local building official who can tell you if such a review is required.

ABOUT THE DESIGNS

The architects and designers whose work appears in this publication are among America's leading residential designers. Each plan was designed to meet the requirements of a nationally recognized model building code in effect at the time and place the plan was drawn. Because national building codes change from time to time, plans may not comply with any such code at the time they are sold to a customer. In addition, building officials may not accept these plans as final construction documents of record as the plans may need to be modified and additional drawings and details added to suit local conditions and requirements. We strongly advise that purchasers consult a licensed architect or engineer, and their local building official, before starting any construction related to these plans.

LOCAL BUILDING CODES AND ZONING REQUIREMENTS

At the time of creation, our plans are drawn to specifications published by the Building Officials and Code Administrators (BOCA) International, Inc.; the Southern Building Code Congress (SBCCI) International, Inc.; the International Conference of Building Officials (ICBO); or the Council of American Building Officials (CABO). Our plans are designed to meet or exceed national building standards. Because of the great differences in geography and climate throughout the United States and Canada, each state, county and municipality has its own building codes, zone requirements, ordinances and building regulations. Your plan may need to be modified to comply with local requirements regarding snow loads, energy codes, soil and seismic conditions and a wide range of other matters. In addition, you may need to obtain permits or inspections from local governments before and in the course of construction. Prior to using blueprints ordered from us, we strongly advise that you consult a licensed architect or engineer—and speak with your local building official—before applying for any permit or beginning construction. We authorize the use of our blueprints on the express condition that you strictly comply with all local building codes, zoning requirements and other applicable laws, regulations, ordinances and requirements. **Notice: Plans for homes to be built in Nevada must be re-drawn by a Nevada-registered professional. Consult your building official for more information on this subject.**

FOUNDATION AND EXTERIOR WALL CHANGES

Depending on your specific climate or regional building practices, you may wish to change a full basement to a slab or crawlspace foundation. Most professional contractors and builders can easily adapt your plans to alternate foundation types. Likewise, most can easily change 2x4 wall construction to 2x6, or vice versa.

DISCLAIMER

We and the designers we work with have put substantial care and effort into the creation of our blueprints. However, because we cannot provide on-site consultation, supervision and control over actual construction, and because of the great variance in local building requirements, building practices and soil, seismic, weather and other conditions, WE CANNOT MAKE ANY WARRANTY, EXPRESS OR IMPLIED, WITH RESPECT TO THE CONTENT OR USE OF OUR BLUEPRINTS, INCLUDING BUT NOT LIMITED TO ANY WARRANTY OF MERCHANTABILITY OR OF FITNESS FOR A PARTICULAR PURPOSE.

TERMS AND CONDITIONS

These designs are protected under the terms of United States Copyright Law and may not be copied or reproduced in any way, by any means, unless you have purchased Sepias or Reproducibles which clearly indicate your right to copy or reproduce. We authorize the use of your chosen design as an aid in the construction of one single family home only. You may not use this design to build a second or multiple dwellings without purchasing another blueprint or blueprints or paying additional design fees.

HOW MANY BLUEPRINTS DO YOU NEED?

A single set of blueprints is sufficient to study a home in greater detail. However, if you are planning to obtain cost estimates from a contractor or subcontractors—or if you are planning to build immediately—you will need more sets. Because additional sets are cheaper when ordered in quantity with the original order, make sure you order enough blueprints to satisfy all requirements. The following checklist will help you determine how many you need:

___ Owner

___ Builder (generally requires at least three sets; one as a legal document, one to use during inspections, and at least one to give to subcontractors)

___ Local Building Department (often requires two sets)

___ Mortgage Lender (usually one set for a conventional loan; three sets for FHA or VA loans)

___ TOTAL NUMBER OF SETS

Have You Seen Our Newest Designs?

At least 50 of our latest creations are featured in each edition of our New Design Portfolio. You may have received a copy with your latest purchase by mail. If not, or if you purchased this book from a local retailer, just return the coupon below for your FREE copy. Make sure you consider the very latest of what Home Planners has to offer.

Yes! Please send my FREE copy of your latest New Design Portfolio.

Offer good to U.S. shipping address only.

Name _____

Address_____

City_____State _____Zip _____

HOME PLANNERS, LLC
Wholly owned by Hanley-Wood, LLC
3275 WEST INA ROAD, SUITE 110
TUCSON, ARIZONA 85741

Order Form Key

HPT464

 TOLL FREE 1-800-521-6797

REGULAR OFFICE HOURS:
8:00 a.m.-12:00 a.m. EST, Monday-Friday, 10:00 a.m.-7:00 p.m. EST Sat & Sun.

If we receive your order by 3:00 p.m. EST, Monday-Friday, we'll process it and ship within **two business days**. When ordering by phone, please have your credit card ready. We'll also ask you for the Order Form Key Number at the bottom of the coupon.

By FAX: Copy the Order Form on the next page and send it on our FAX line: 1-800-224-6699 or 520-544-3086.

Canadian Customers — Order Toll Free 1-877-223-6389

For faster service, Canadian customers may now call in orders directly to our Canadian supplier of plans and charge the purchase to a credit card. Or, you may complete the order form at right, adding the current exchange rate to all prices and mail in Canadian funds to:

Home Planners Canada, c/o Select Home Designs
301-611 Alexander Street • Vancouver, BC, Canada • V6A 1E1

OR: Copy the Order Form and send it via our FAX line: 1-800-224-6699.

ORDER FORM

The Home Customizer®

"This house is perfect...if only the family room were two feet wider." Sound familiar? In response to the numerous requests for this type of modification, Home Planners has developed **The Home Customizer® Package**. This exclusive package offers our top-of-the-line materials to make it easy for anyone, anywhere to customize any Home Planners design to fit their needs. Check the index on page 138-139 for those plans which are customizable.

Some of the changes you can make to any of our plans include:

- exterior elevation changes
- kitchen and bath modifications
- roof, wall and foundation changes
- room additions and more!

The Home Customizer® Package includes everything you'll need to make the necessary changes to your favorite Home Planners design. The package includes:

- instruction book with examples
- architectural scale and clear work film
- erasable red marker and removable correction tape
- ¼"-scale furniture cutouts
- 1 set reproducible drawings
- 1 set study blueprints for communicating changes to your design professional
- a copyright release letter so you can make copies as you need them
- referral letter with the name, address and telephone number of the professional in your region who is trained in modifying Home Planners designs efficiently and inexpensively.

The Home Customizer® Package will not only save you 25% to 75% of the cost of drawing the plans from scratch with an architect or engineer, it will also give you the flexibility to have your changes and modifications made by our referral network or by the professional of your choice. Now it's even easier and more affordable to have the custom home you've always wanted.

ORDER TOLL FREE!
FOR INFORMATION ABOUT ANY OF OUR SERVICES OR TO ORDER CALL

1-800-521-6797 OR 520-297-8200
Browse our website:
www.eplans.com

BLUEPRINTS ARE NOT REFUNDABLE
EXCHANGES ONLY

FOR CUSTOMER SERVICE,
CALL TOLL FREE **1-888-690-1116.**

HOME PLANNERS, LLC wholly owned by Hanley-Wood, LLC
3275 WEST INA ROAD, SUITE 110 • TUCSON, ARIZONA • 85741

THE BASIC BLUEPRINT PACKAGE
Rush me the following (please refer to the Plans Index and Price Schedule in this section):
___Set(s) of blueprints for plan number(s) _____. $_____
___Set(s) of reproducibles for plan number(s) _____. $_____
___Home Customizer® Package for plan(s)_____. $_____
___Additional identical blueprints (standard or reverse) in same order @ $50 per set. $_____
___Reverse blueprints @ $50 fee per order. Right-reading reverse @ $165 surcharge $_____

IMPORTANT EXTRAS
Rush me the following:
___Materials List: $60 (Must be purchased with Blueprint set.) Add $10 for Schedule C4–L4 plans. $_____
___**Quote One®** Summary Cost Report @ $29.95 for one, $14.95 for each additional,
    for plans _____ $_____
    Building location: City _____ Zip Code _____
___**Quote One®** Materials Cost Report @ $120 Schedules P1–C3; $130 Schedules C4–L4,
    for plan_____(Must be purchased with Blueprints set.) $_____
    Building location: City _____ Zip Code _____
___Specification Outlines @ $10 each. $_____
___Detail Sets @ $14.95 each; any two $22.95; any three $29.95; all four for $39.95 (save $19.85). $_____
    ❑ Plumbing ❑ Electrical ❑ Construction ❑ Mechanical
___Plan-A-Home® @ $29.95 each. $_____

DECK BLUEPRINTS
(Please refer to the Plans Index and Price Schedule in this section)
___Set(s) of Deck Plan _____. $_____
___Additional identical blueprints in same order @ $10 per set. $_____
___Reverse blueprints @ $10 per set. $_____
___Set of Standard Deck Details @ $14.95 per set. $_____
___Set of Complete Deck Construction Package (Best Buy!) Add $10 to Building Package
    Includes Custom Deck Plan _____ Plus Standard Deck Details

LANDSCAPE BLUEPRINTS
(Please refer to the Plans Index and Price Schedule in this section)
___Set(s) of Landscape Plan _____. $_____
___Additional identical blueprints in same order @ $10 per set. $_____
___Reverse blueprints @ $10 per set. $_____
Please indicate the appropriate region of the country for Plant & Material List.
(See map on page 137): Region _____

POSTAGE AND HANDLING	1–3 sets	4+ sets
Signature is required for all deliveries. **DELIVERY** No CODs (Requires street address—No P.O. Boxes)		
•Regular Service (Allow 7–10 business days delivery)	❑ $20.00	❑ $25.00
•Priority (Allow 4–5 business days delivery)	❑ $25.00	❑ $35.00
•Express (Allow 3 business days delivery)	❑ $35.00	❑ $45.00
OVERSEAS DELIVERY	fax, phone or mail for quote	

Note: All delivery times are from date Blueprint Package is shipped.

POSTAGE (From box above) $_____
SUBTOTAL $_____
SALES TAX (AZ & MI residents, please add appropriate state and local sales tax.) $_____
TOTAL (Subtotal and tax) $_____

YOUR ADDRESS (please print)

Name _____

Street_____

City _____State_____Zip _____

Daytime telephone number (_____) _____

FOR CREDIT CARD ORDERS ONLY

Credit card number _____ Exp. Date: (M/Y) _____
Check one ❑ Visa ❑ MasterCard ❑ Discover Card ❑ American Express

Signature_____

Please check appropriate box: ❑ Licensed Builder-Contractor ❑ Homeowner

ORDER TOLL FREE!
1-800-521-6797 or 520-297-8200

Order Form Key

HPT464

HOME PLANNERS WANTS YOUR BUILDING EXPERIENCE TO BE AS PLEASANT AND TROUBLE-FREE AS POSSIBLE.

That's why we've expanded our library of Do-It-Yourself titles to help you along. In addition to our beautiful plans books, we've added books to guide you through specific projects as well as the construction process. In fact, these are titles that will be as useful after your dream home is built as they are right now.

BIGGEST & BEST

1001 of our best-selling plans in one volume. 1,074 to 7,275 square feet. 704 pgs $12.95 1K1

ONE-STORY

450 designs for all lifestyles. 800 to 4,900 square feet. 384 pgs $9.95 OS

MORE ONE-STORY

475 superb one-level plans from 800 to 5,000 square feet. 448 pgs $9.95 MOS

TWO-STORY

443 designs for one-and-a-half and two stories. 1,500 to 6,000 square feet. 448 pgs $9.95 TS

VACATION

465 designs for recreation, retirement and leisure. 448 pgs $9.95 VSH

HILLSIDE

208 designs for split-levels, bi-levels, multi-levels and walkouts. 224 pgs $9.95 HH

FARMHOUSE

200 country designs from classic to contemporary by 7 winning designers. 224 pgs $8.95 FH

COUNTRY HOUSES

208 unique home plans that combine traditional style and modern livability. 224 pgs $9.95 CN

BUDGET-SMART

200 efficient plans from 7 top designers, that you can really afford to build! 224 pgs $8.95 BS

BARRIER FREE

Over 1,700 products and 51 plans for accessible living. 128 pgs $15.95 UH

ENCYCLOPEDIA

500 exceptional plans for all styles and budgets—the best book of its kind! 528 pgs $9.95 ENC

ENCYCLOPEDIA II

500 completely new plans. Spacious and stylish designs for every budget and taste. 352 pgs $9.95 E2

AFFORDABLE

Completely revised and updated, featuring 300 designs for modest budgets. 256 pgs $9.95 AF

VICTORIAN

NEW! 210 striking Victorian and Farmhouse designs from today's top designers. 224 pgs $15.95 VDH2

ESTATE

Dream big! Twenty-one designers showcase their biggest and best plans. 208 pgs $15.95 EDH

LUXURY

154 fine luxury plans—loaded with luscious amenities! 192 pgs $14.95 LD2

EUROPEAN STYLES

200 homes with a unique flair of the Old World. 224 pgs $15.95 EURO

COUNTRY CLASSICS

Donald Gardner's 101 best Country and Traditional home plans. 192 pgs $17.95 DAG

WILLIAM POOLE
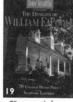
70 romantic house plans that capture the classic tradition of home design. 160 pgs $17.95 WEP

TRADITIONAL

85 timeless designs from the Design Traditions Library. 160 pgs $17.95 TRA

COTTAGES

25 fresh new designs that are as warm as a tropical breeze. A blend of the best aspects of many coastal styles. 64 pgs. $19.95 CTG

CLASSIC

Timeless, elegant designs that always feel like home. Gorgeous plans that are as flexible and up-to-date as their occupants. 240 pgs. $9.95 CS

CONTEMPORARY

The most complete and imaginative collection of contemporary designs available anywhere. 240 pgs. $9.95 CM

EASY-LIVING

200 efficient and sophisticated plans that are small in size, but big on livability. 224 pgs $8.95 EL

SOUTHERN

207 homes rich in Southern styling and comfort. 240 pgs $8.95 SH

SOUTHWESTERN

138 designs that capture the spirit of the Southwest. 144 pgs $10.95 SW

WESTERN

215 designs that capture the spirit and diversity of the Western lifestyle. 208 pgs $9.95 WH

NEIGHBORHOOD

170 designs with the feel of main street America. 192 pgs $12.95 TND

CRAFTSMAN

170 Home plans in the Craftsman and Bungalow style. 192 pgs $12.95 CC

COLONIAL HOUSES

181 Classic early American designs. 208 pgs $9.95 COL

DUPLEX & TOWNHOMES

Over 50 designs for multi-family living. 64 pgs $9.95 DTP

WATERFRONT

200 designs perfect for your waterside wonderland. 208 pgs $10.95 WF

  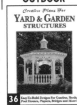    

   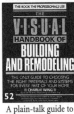    

Design 2875, page 63

OVER 3 MILLION BLUEPRINTS SOLD

"We instructed our builder to follow the plans including all of the many details which make this house so elegant…Our home is a fine example of the results one can achieve by purchasing and following the plans which you offer…Everyone who has seen it has assured us that it belongs in 'a picture book.' I truly mean it when I say that my home 'is a DREAM HOUSE.'"

S.P.
Anderson, SC

"We have had a steady stream of visitors, many of whom tell us this is the most beautiful home they've seen. Everyone is amazed at the layout and remarks on how unique it is. Our real estate attorney, who is a Chicago dweller and who deals with highly valued properties, told me this is the only suburban home he has seen that he would want to live in."

W. & P.S.
Flossmoor, IL

"Your blueprints saved us a great deal of money. I acted as the general contractor and we did a lot of the work ourselves. We probably built it for half the cost! We are thinking about more plans for another home. I purchased a competitor's book but my husband wants only your plans!"

K.M.
Grovetown, GA

"We are very happy with the product of our efforts. The neighbors and passersby appreciate what we have created. We have had many people stop by to discuss our house and kindly praise it as being the nicest house in our area of new construction. We have even had one person stop and make us an unsolicited offer to buy the house for much more than we have invested in it."

K. & L.S.
Bolingbrook, IL

"The traffic going past our house is unbelievable. On several occasions, we have heard that it is the 'prettiest house in Batvia.' Also, when meeting someone new and mentioning what street we live on, quite often we're told, 'Oh, you're the one in the yellow house with the wrap-around porch! I love it!'"

A.W.
Batvia, NY

"I have been involved in the building trades my entire life…Since building our home we have built two other homes for other families. Their plans from local professional architects were not nearly as good as yours. For that reason we are ordering additional plan books from you."

T.F.
Kingston, WA

"The blueprints we received from you were of excellent quality and provided us with exactly what we needed to get our successful home-building project underway. We appreciate your invaluable role in our home-building effort."

T.A.
Concord, TN